Overcon

Anxiety

A Step by Step Guide and Proven Techniques on How to Use Psychological Triggers and Dark Psychology Secrets to Understand How to Stop Worrying and Stop Anxiety

Mark Panic

Table of Contents

Introduction

Are you suffering from Social Anxiety Disorder (SAD)? Do you dread meeting new people, going to a party, or even eating a meal in public? Do you fear being embarrassed or humiliated in front of others or think people can sense your nervousness? Can you recognize the symptoms of this disorder in yourself or in someone that you know?

In this book, Overcoming Social Anxiety*: A Step by Step Guide and Proven Techniques on How to Use Psychological Triggers and Dark Psychology Secrets to Understand How to Stop Worrying and Stop Anxiety,* you will learn exactly what social anxiety disorder is, how it affects those who suffer from it, and how severely it can impact on their lives.

Social anxiety disorder is the intense anxiety of being judged, evaluated negatively, rejected in social situations, and watched by others that brings about a persistent, powerful fear.

SAD affects school, work, and everyday activities. Friendships may be hard to make and keep. People with SAD may suffer from alcohol and drug abuse because they self-medicate to try to work through the condition.

The hard part of having this condition is having the ability to ask for help.

This book is written to help people identify if they have a social anxiety disorder or if there is someone you know who does and to benefit from the resources provided to help in dealing with this mental condition that may be preventing you to cope with the condition and to prevent it from being psychologically harmful.

How to Get the Most Out of this Book

This book has been written to work in several ways:

- o To read this book in its entirety to ensure you understand and derive all you need to know about social anxiety disorder, excessive worrying and the treatments that can help those who need help managing their condition

- o To learn the causes and reasons of SAD and how it affects those who suffer from it

- o To use this book as a guide to help you review and reread portions of the book that you feel may pertain to you or someone you know

This book is written to be instructional and informative. Some of the information may be, for some people, unbelievable and may wonder how someone deals with their social anxiety, especially if it is extreme.

People who deal with SAD on a daily basis have everything in the lives affected. The probability of not being able to maintain a job, eat a meal in a restaurant or attend a party all while dealing with sometimes crippling fear, anxiety, depression, and much more.

However, once you read about what this disorder is about and how a person deals with their condition and the options there are for treatment, it will become more understandable.

This book has been written in the hopes that you learn about social anxiety disorder, and if you or someone you know is affected, can have a better understanding of the disorder and help manage it.

Chapter 1: Understanding Social Anxiety Disorder

Do you have an extreme fear of having others judge you? Do you feel self-conscious while in common, everyday social situations? Are you uncomfortable or fear meeting new people and avoid doing so if you can?

If you find that you identify with some of the situations mentioned or you know of someone who is suffering from a social anxiety disorder, this chapter will define what the disorder is, and explain how it impacts those who live with a social anxiety disorder and those around them.

These feeling can make it hard for you to go about your day like talking to people at school or work if you've been having these feelings for at least six months or more. The feelings you are having may be that you're suffering from a social anxiety disorder.

Also called social phobia, social anxiety disorder is one of the most common of mental health disorders after substance abuse and depression.

Social anxiety disorder is the intense anxiety of being judged, evaluated negatively, rejected in social situations, and watched by others which bring about a persistent, powerful fear.

This affects your school, work, and everyday activities. Friendships may be hard to make and keep. The hard part of having this condition is having the ability to ask for help.

How Many People are Afflicted with Social Anxiety Disorder?

Social anxiety disorder (SAD) affects approximately 15 million adults in the United States.

Research shows that 48% of the American population has some degree of shyness while extreme shyness leans more towards social anxiety disorder. The disorder is found equally afflicting women and men and usually begins at about 13 years of age.

Almost 50 percent of all people who are diagnosed with SAD are also prone to and diagnosed with depression. Other effects of social anxiety disorder are negative thoughts, poor social skills that lack improvement, sensitivity to criticism, and low self-esteem.

Although there are treatments that are available and have been shown to be effective, less than 5 percent of people with SAD actually seek treatment within the first year after the onset of the disorder. Additionally, more than a third of people who have had symptoms delay getting treatment for more than 10 years.

People who have an extreme fear of finding themselves in social situations and feel so fearful to the point of panic are suffering from a social anxiety disorder.

For those who are always open to social events, dining out, eating meals with others, speaking in front of an audience, or even interacting with a small group, this disorder can be puzzling, even off-putting at times.

However, those who suffer this disorder tend to avoid social situations because it brings up extreme and overwhelming anxiety. Although a person with this disorder will side-step most social events, it's not realistically feasible to be able to hide out forever.

People with this disorder worry about appearing anxious (tripping over their words or blushing) or being thought of as boring, awkward, or stupid. Because of this phobia, they frequently avoid social situations, and when they can't avoid them, react with a great amount of distress and anxiety. Many even experience physical symptoms such as nausea and sweating. They may even have full-blown attacks of anxiety.

They can't avoid events that will put them in social situations like dining out and eating in front of others or attending holiday functions with family. There will also be times when they will have to speak in front of others, like making client presentations, for example, or offering some words of welcome to a new staff member or a newcomer to their community.

Today, there is new research that is now showing how social anxiety disorder is more than just its symptoms. This chapter will cover what the symptoms are and discuss how to understand what this disorder is.

There have been two views by researchers about social anxiety disorder. One view is that you either have it or you don't (known by researchers as a discrete categorical entity). The other view is that the more social situations a person fears and avoids, the more harmed, reclusive, and impaired the person becomes.

However, researchers now believe these two views are faulty. They now believe that SAD is a developing phenomenon that comes from connecting interactions among symptoms. This means that a person with SAD does not have one or two or five situations where they fear (their) public behavior.

All the situations group together in ways that are related and forming a "network" of situations. The network may be the fear of going to a party or meeting strangers or calling people you may only slightly know. These fears are social situations that are new and are different than, for example, fear of taking a test, or returning or exchanging

something to a department store.
(Whitbourne Ph.D., 2018)

Social Anxiety Disorder – What it's Like to Suffer from It

People who suffer from SAD talk about how afraid they are when they attended school. They didn't want to be called upon by their teacher, not because they didn't know the answer, because usually, they did. Their fear was based on how they thought other students would think about them. They feared they would be thought of as boring or stupid.

Getting a job and talking to their manager or having to speak in a meeting is a problem for people with a social anxiety disorder. They may be the smartest person in the room, but no one would know it because of their fear of interacting and inability to talk.

People need to calm themselves with several alcoholic drinks when attending a social function like a wedding or a holiday party because of their fear to meet and talk to new people.

In time, some people turned to drink every day in order to face the day and try to control their fears. Finally realizing that drinking isn't the answer, they consult with a medical professional and a counselor to realistically cope with their fears.

Understanding Social Anxiety

The most important step to not feeling unaware or lost about when and why you feel social anxiety is to understand it. Having the answers to these questions will help to understand the symptoms and their impact on the condition.

The fear of being judged – what is it called? - The fear of being judged is called *sociophobia*.

Is social anxiety considered a mental disorder? – Social anxiety is a complicated group of behaviors, thoughts, and emotions that can cause a person to suffer from the fears and anxieties that are linked to this disorder.

A group of behaviors, thoughts, and emotions can be referred to as a disorder or a syndrome. To classify and study complex conditions is why psychiatrists and researchers use the word *disorder*. (Hamilton, 2019)

Social Anxiety Disorder – What Are the Symptoms?

Avoiding social situations and powerful anxiety while in social situations are the two key symptoms of social anxiety. Many people who have this disorder don't realize what happens to them but have feelings of things just not being right.

A person may be aware that they are feeling unreasonable fear but can't seem to overcome it. They have fears of looking bad, feel humiliated or embarrassed, or will make mistakes in front of other people.

These fears illuminate the possible twisted thinking of these individuals. Their thoughts about the negative opinions of others and false beliefs about social situations have a problem recognizing the true opinions of others and how social situations are not set up for the judgment of others.

Another form of this type of anxiety is known as *anticipatory anxiety*. People with this type of anxiety suffer from fear of an event that is scheduled to happen days or even weeks before the actual event.

Other symptoms of social anxiety can be physical. *These physical conditions can include sweating, shaking, upset stomach, a pounding heart, and muscle tension* to name a few of the physical reactions that a person with SAD may have.

Social anxiety in children may be expressed by crying, having a tantrum, or adhering to a parent.

Extreme social anxiety can turn into a panic attack. Sudden onset of an anxiety attack can reach a maximum peak within minutes. Some of the following symptoms may accompany an attack – sweating, shaking or trembling, shortness of breath or feelings of being smothered, heart palpitations/increased heart rate, chest pains, nausea, dizziness, and feelings of unreality. (Hamilton, 2019)

A person with social anxiety symptoms may feel severe distress experiencing several social situations and having suffered some of the physical symptoms mentioned will probably avoid them.

People with SAD have fears about specific situations, such as meeting new people, yet there is more than one fear that most people with SAD have.

 (Hamilton, 2019)

Situations That Provoke Social Anxiety

- Entering a room in front of others
- Speaking to a stranger
- Being the center of attention
- Eating or drinking in front of others
- Typing while someone stands over them
- Performing a job while being watched
- Speaking in a classroom or a meeting
- Going to parties
- Job interviews
- Taking a test
- Going on a date
- Using a public restroom

How Social Anxiety Disorder Manifests in Different Ways

There are many more situations that can provoke social anxiety that is subject to an individual's feelings and fears. An example is a young girl who drapes a napkin over her mouth and sandwich because she feels "embarrassed" about eating and chewing her food in front of her classmates.

This action seems strange to other children who have no anxiety connected to eating in front of others. Unfortunately, making fun of the girl exacerbates the situation, embarrassing her even more.

Another example of a person with a social anxiety disorder is a businesswoman with a successful career and just got engaged to be married. She attended the best schools, is attractive, and her colleagues see her as a caring and kind individual, always with a smile and a greeting.

Her social anxiety disorder isn't obvious to those around her. But in group settings, she shies away from participating in discussions and rather prefers to blend into the background.

If spoken to directly, she tends to stammer and choke up, sometimes tripping over her own words. When she has to make a presentation to a client, she has feelings of nausea and can only get through it by having a drink or two beforehand.

There are some situations that may not cause problems for one person but will wreak havoc of unease and anxiety for another. A person with SAD may have no problem giving a lecture to an audience but attending a party can be a nightmare for them.

When does it happen?

When a person has a social anxiety disorder, situations that are stressful are too much to handle. Anything from meeting new people and making eye contact and small talk to eating a meal in front of people can make a person feel uncomfortable. These are aspects of life that can create anxious moments for a person with SAD. (WebMD, 2019)

Social anxiety disorder is not a choice – People suffering from SAD actually wish they could be like everyone else. What is so simple and normal for other people can affect a person so adversely they can become physically ill. (Holmes, 2015)

Family and friends find SAD hard to understand – The social anxiety disorder isn't easy for family and friends to understand. Immediate family members – parents and siblings – quietly accept the disorder because they live with the person and see it every day. It may not be as pronounced at home because there is a familiarity with the family. (Holmes, 2015)

Making friends and keeping friends is hard – It's difficult to meet new people and make friends. When a person with SAD does make friends, it can be hard to keep the friendship going. Socializing with others can be a chore and you can't stay home avoiding parties and various social events all the time.

A person with SAD can't just stop suffering from it – Social anxiety disorder is not like a cold. There isn't medicine that can be taken and it goes away. Being asked "is there anything you can take" or "just get over it" is not easy to hear and frustrating to those who suffer from it. It's not that simple.

Understanding and Compassion are welcomed - Social anxiety is extremely debilitating for those who suffer from the disorder. Any overture that remotely seems like understanding or compassion is welcomed.

People with a SAD wish that people, especially those who are the closest to them, would read information and links to articles that are sent to them so they could have a better understanding of how the SAD brain works. They would know how texting is easier for a person with SAD than talking on the phone or how it feels better to go to a dinner party at the home of close friends that they are familiar with rather than going out to a public restaurant.

Social anxiety can be unpredictable – Some people with SAD have instances when they don't feel the fear or anxiousness that comes with the disorder. However, there are other times that it comes up out of nowhere.

People with social anxiety order can be misunderstood. They can, at times, have a fun time with close friends and will want to spend time with them, and other times, they won't pick up the phone and avoid the same friends altogether if it involves new people being introduced into the group.

Although they can seem perfectly normal at times doesn't mean that there isn't a continued struggle with this disorder.

Meeting people isn't easy – Making friends and meeting new people at an event can be really difficult for people with social anxiety. There are people who suffer from SAD who decline social events such as dinner out if they know there will be new people to meet. Some friends will try to understand, while others move on.

Shyness and social anxiety disorder are not the same things – Shyness is a temporary condition that, as time passes and the person becomes more comfortable with others and situations, the shyness will eventually disappear.

Social anxiety disorder is a mental condition that prevents a person from meeting new people or having a simple discussion with another person. (Holmes, Lindsay, 2015)

Social anxiety disorder can affect otherwise normal situations – People with SAD can have otherwise normal situations be destroyed because of their condition. Some may decline a job offer that entails interacting with new people, while some may have a hard time completing courses at school, show up for an interview, or even have the possibility of a romantic relationship.

Self-medication - Another situation that can impact negatively on some people with SAD is drug and alcohol abuse. In order to overcome the impact of the anxiousness that a person feels in the situations that make them feel uncomfortable, they self-medicate with drugs and alcohol to "handle" the situation.

Social anxiety disorder for those who are caught in its web is debilitating, frustrating, and can affect a person in so many negative ways. Their quality of life is impacted; they are not comfortable in many social situations that most of us glide through without a thought on a daily basis.

Job opportunities, friendships, family social events, eating a meal, walking into a room, and so many other things can provoke a person to feel the fear of being judged. This is unthinkable to those who do not subscribe to these types of feelings but is a nightmare begin lived with on a daily basis by a person who suffers from SAD.

There is still quite a bit to cover on this topic as well as how it leads to other side-effects. The following chapter will cover what actually causes social anxiety disorder. When and how it takes hold of a person and what provocations may have begun the spiral of this condition getting out of control.

Chapter 2: What Causes Social Anxiety Disorder

There are several reasons as to what actually causes social anxiety disorder. An exact one cannot be the definitive reason. If you have had a diagnosis of social anxiety disorder, you may have had some thoughts as to where did it come from, or how you developed this illness. Realize no one factor is the reason, but a combined interplay of various situations that have resulted in this disorder.

The answer is a complicated **combination of psychological, biological, and environmental elements. There is no one thing that causes this disorder.**

Genetics and SAD

Genetics may be one of the factors. If there is a family member, such as a parent who is considered a first-degree relative, has a social disorder, the possibility is that a person may also be two to six times more likely to be at risk of having it as well. Estimates show from research that approximately 30 to 40 percent or one-third of causes of SAD are derived from a person's genetics.

Another factor may be a person having an overactive amygdala, where the fear response is housed in the brain. Social anxiety disorder is associated with brain circuits functioning unusually. These circuits are ones that regulate fear and the response in the brain of *fight or flight*.

As stated in Chapter 1, social anxiety disorder usually manifests at about the age of 13. There may be a connection between abuse, bullying, or teasing. Kids who are shy in their younger years have a tendency to become adults that are socially anxious.

Children who are a product of controlling, overbearing parents can also have anxiety issues as well. Being sheltered or overprotected by their parents may not give the child an opportunity to learn good, healthy social skills as part of their development. Additionally, anything that points to a child's appearance, voice, or health condition can become a trigger of social anxiety as well.

Observing the behavior of adults as a child or seeing how others were treated as a result of their behavior, like being humiliated, ridiculed, or laughed at can cause a chile to develop their fears.

Not wanting to be treated in the same way, they shy away from expressing themselves or even interacting with others fearing they'll be judged by behaving in a certain manner. (Cuncic MA, 2019)

Environmental Causes and SAD

Causes of a social anxiety disorder include environmental factors that affect you as you grow up. You are more likely to develop social anxiety disorder if one of your parents has a social anxiety disorder.

Theories have been developed by psychologists that children may develop to become socially anxious through learning it in various ways.

How a Child Learns Social Anxiety

Observing – Did you see another person in a social situation that was traumatic? Someone who is already susceptible to the disorder, even though they have not experienced a traumatic situation themselves, may have a traumatic situation experienced by another person as experiencing the situation firsthand.

Direct experience – Did you have other kids bully or tease you, push you physically, or make fun of you? Were you smarter than the other kids and were excluded from a group because you won all the class awards?

Although these experiences are not necessarily triggers, having early traumatic events may have an impact on the child and on the development of their social anxiety, sometimes, in later years.

Informational experience – Children, whose parents who are socially anxious and fearful, receive non-verbal and verbal information transferred unwittingly by their parents. The information the child receives is usually about the risks of social situations. For example, if your parents always worried about what kind of house you lived in or the car they drove and drew comparisons to others in their neighborhood, it may well be that you developed some of the same worries and anxieties.

How you were brought up as a child also impacts on the possibility that you will develop or already have a social anxiety disorder. The likelihood you will or have developed the disorder is:

You were not exposed to social situations on a routine basis as a child and were not allowed to develop suitable social skills.

One or both parents were overprotective, critical, or controlling. Children who do not form a good connection to their main caregiver are more at a risk because they can't soothe and calm themselves when they are in anxious situations. (Cuncic MA, 2019)

Childhood Inhibition

Have you ever seen a toddler or young child get extremely upset when they are challenged with a person who is unfamiliar to them, or a new situation, like their parents visiting friends the child has never seen before? When these situations happen, does the child turn to "hide" and seek comfort from their parent? Do they withdraw or cry?

Behavioral inhibition is what this type of behavior is. It is when children show inhibition in their behavior as a toddler or young child. This type of behavior makes a toddler at greater risk to develop SAD in later life.

Temperament begins to reveal itself at a young age and can be a characteristic that is inborn and the effect of biological factors.

Parents are encouraged to consult with a professional if they are concerned that their child is fearful or withdrawn excessively. This kind of behavior exhibited by toddlers and young children is a call for concern. It is more than likely that if a child exhibits behavioral inhibition, they need intervention at an early age to possibly prevent a more serious problem in the future.

Biological and Brain Structure

Neuroimaging is a technique that can create a picture of the brain. Just as x-rays can see the inner skeletal of the body, the same can be done to the brain. State of the art techniques can not only look at the structure of the brain but can also see the different types of functions in individual regions of the brain.

Researchers may look at blood flow and their differences in specific areas of the brain for mental disorders and for people who have a specific disorder.

There are four areas of the brain that are impacted when you experience anxiety:

- ○ Brain stem – heart rate and breathing are controlled by this area

- ○ Limbic system – your mood and anxiety level are affected. The *amygdala* is part of the limbic system and is associated with fear

- o Motor cortex – your muscles are controlled by this area of the brain

- o Prefrontal cortex – risk and danger are assessed by this part of the brain

A study of blood flow in the brain discovered differences in the brains of people who suffered from social phobia when they spoke in public. A type of neuroimaging called *Positron Emission Tomography (PET)* was used for this study. (Cuncic MA, 2019
The images supplied by PET exhibited that people with SAD showed an increase of blood flow in the amygdala, the area of the brain associated with fear and a part of the limbic system.

A comparison of PET images of people without SAD showed an increase of blood flow to the cerebral cortex, the area of the brain associated with evaluation and thinking.

The comparison of the two groups showed the brain reacts differently to social situations by people with SAD than people who do not have the disorder.

The Brain and Neurotransmitters

There are likely particular chemical imbalances in your brain, known as neurotransmitters if you have a social anxiety disorder. Neurotransmitters are used by the brain and send indicators and signals from one cell to another.

The neurotransmitters involved in anxiety are:

Norepinephrine – is similar to adrenaline and also called noradrenaline. Your heart rate and blood pressure soar during a "fight or flight" reaction. An unexpected increase in norepinephrine can lead to panic attacks.

Dopamine – dopamine functions as a neurotransmitter in the brain. Its two main functions are movement and motivation. It also has cognitive functions such as focus and memory.

Serotonin – this neurotransmitter relays messages from one area of the brain to another. The brain cells that are related to appetite, sleep, memory, learning, mood, sexual desire, temperature regulation, and some social behaviors are affected by serotonin.

Gamma-aminobutyric acid (GABA) – an amino acid in the body acting in the central nervous system as a neurotransmitter. The lack of the correct levels of GABA in the body activates nerve cells too frequently causing mental illnesses worse such as social anxiety disorder, post-traumatic stress disorder (PTSD and depression).

People with SAD display some of the similar imbalances of these neurotransmitters as people who suffer from *agoraphobia* (a type of anxiety disorder where you fear and avoid places that may cause panic, a feeling of being trapped, helpless, or embarrassed) and *panic disorder*.

There is no single cause of SAD. Most people display the disorder as a result of a complex number of factors. In order to treat SAD, a doctor or mental health professional will work with someone and discuss other factors that have contributed to their social anxieties. (Cuncic MA, 2019)

Other Causes of Social Anxiety Disorder

Now that you know there are a complex number of reasons that can cause a social anxiety disorder that began when you were a child or young adult, there are other causes that have to do with other negative thought processes.

Low self-esteem – some of the symptoms of low self-esteem are:

- Social withdrawal
- Sensitivity to criticism
- Putting on a "false" front for others

Trouble being assertive – when you are assertive, you tell someone what you're thinking, wanting, or wishing. This is simple in theory and on paper, but for someone with SAD who has problems being assertive, this is not easy to achieve.

The reasons that being assertive is difficult can be:

The fear of being disconnected with the other person – worrying about how the other person will feel and if they get upset will create distance between you.

You have low self-worth – this goes hand-in-hand with low self-esteem. You believe you don't deserve to have a voice or have it heard. Combined with a social anxiety disorder, you have a problem being heard, or stumble over your words and feel embarrassed and judged.

Negative Self-Talk

The phrase *"we are our own worst critics"* is magnified when you have SAD. Couple social anxiety disorder with talking to ourselves negatively is a toxic situation of your own making.

There are many forms of negative self-talk. It can be "I'm not really good at this so for my own safety, *I'm not going to continue doing this"* to being mean to yourself by saying *"I can't say or do anything right!"*

This is the *inner-critic* that you allow to negatively self-talk. If you are already dealing with social anxiety disorder and have a fear of being judged or looked upon negatively, you do the exact thing that you fear when you talk negatively about yourself, about your abilities, never using encouraging, supportive words or phrases.

The toll of negative self-talk can have a pretty damaging impact. Higher levels of stress and low levels of self-esteem are linked to negative self-talk.

Decreased motivation, greater feelings of helplessness, fear of being judged by others, and negatively judging yourself are all the harmful consequences of negative self-talk.

Poor Social Skills

Social skills are something that you need in navigating through life. Weak people skills can be the result of inborn and life experience factors.

A combination of these factors impacts how social problems come about. They affect people and lead them to:

- o Lack of self-worth and become more insecure
- o Have doubts about their ability in social situations
- o Become more anxious and worried when they're in social situations

- Learn unhelpful beliefs and social behaviors rather than learning better ones
- Miss opportunities to gain experience in social practices

It's possible that some children have parents that aren't good role models and were unsociable themselves. Maybe they made friends with other kids who are unsociable and they copy this social problem.

A Childhood that was Protected and Sheltered

Some people look to their sheltered childhood and upbringing as a major reason for their social ineptness. During their childhood, they didn't have the opportunity to interact with other kids and practice their social skills or what they learned from their parents wasn't that helpful once they grew up and were out in the world.

Another factor was a person was an only child and were so sheltered that they had difficulties with their social skills later in life.

Parents who were socially anxious and awkward themselves lean towards restricting activities their kids are able to do. It may be that they want to protect their kids from the social world that can be rather daunting and scary. Or, it may be because the parents themselves want to side-step socializing with other parents and families and that is what they would have to do if they allowed their child to get socially involved with other kids.

Being Bullied/Picked On

Someone being bullied or picked on when they were younger presents several factors related to weak or lack of social skills. Bullying can kill the self-esteem of a person and make them feel anxious about future interactions with the person or group who are doing the bullying. Additionally, someone can be left feeling bitter and wary about other people. The trust factor is tested and probably end up being non-existent. Socializing, in general, doesn't exist.

Teasing and picking on a child can make them feel off-balance and confused. They may exhibit social behavior that is inappropriate as ways to stop those who are doing the teasing. An example is to yell or throw objects at the other people in order to fight back at them or get them to go away.

Children can usually be picked on by their peers at school, but they can also feel bullied and put down by their siblings, parents, family relatives, or adult authority figures like teachers.

People who struggle with a SAD state that, as children, they were teased by their older siblings or cousins. Others talk about the treatment they endured from insensitive and unsympathetic coaches or teachers.

Physical Differences

People who grew up with physical differences that were noticeable were usually picked on and made fun of for whatever the physical difference was.

Some were made fun of because of their weight (either overweight or extremely underweight), their height – too tall or too short. Other physical differences are:

- Physical feature that is pronounced – big ears, a lisp, an overbite
- Having extreme acne
- Puberty changes earlier or later than other kids
- Physical disability
- Racially different than the majority of the other kids at school

Children will find anything about other kids that's different and can become a target. Some kids aren't even teased or picked on but don't have self-confidence which may be enough that they feel as if they stand out and that there's something wrong with them.

There is a myriad of reasons as to why kids get picked on. Physical differences become targets, but there are other reasons that they may be singled out and teased by their peers:

- Coming from a poor family
- Their religious beliefs
- Their ethnic background
- If they speak with an accent
- Coming from a family with a "bad" reputation
- Their sexuality
- Interests that may be unpopular with others

People with SAD also relate how their parents and other adults/authority figures chipped away at their self-esteem by picking on them:

Parents harped upon anything from not being like their siblings, not being interested in what they considered the right things and not being outspoken enough.

Authority figures didn't fare any better with their insensitivity by telling a child they're too clumsy or lack athletic ability, were too quiet and did not speak up enough in class.

Some people recalled that their problems were in connection with situations where a coach or teacher embarrassed them in front of their class or team with everyone looking on.

Other Experiences That Destroy Self-Confidence

There are other childhood experiences that people with a SAD mention that impacts their sense of self-worth and confidence and how they related to the people around them.

Being overshadowed by a sibling or friend – people who had a healthy and successful social life left the child discouraged and damaged their self-confidence and self-worth. They felt inferior and felt they could not measure up and compete and gave up.

Tragic Experience During Childhood – a child's parent may pass away and the loss impacts their sense of feeling safe and self-confident. They may understandably become withdrawn during their time of mourning. Some children may even be picked on by classmates because of their quiet and withdrawn demeanor.

Serious abuse – children who are abused, whether emotionally, physically or sexually being brought up in a chaotic, toxic environment or due to neglect can be unbelievably damaged during their formative years. The possibility that their social skills and development are stymied.

Children who have been abused become withdrawn and shy. They may become guarded and distrustful of others and will not share their thoughts and emotions. Their self-esteem may spiral downwards as they consider themselves as worthless and in some way deserving of the abuse they're receiving.

Other children go in the opposite direction and begin to act out, getting into trouble, are disruptive and have angry outbursts. They create a sense of safety and implement an unpredictable, tough *don't mess with me* attitude to chase their peers away.

Abuse can cause the child to develop some severe mental health issues, as well as substance abuse. As they grow to adulthood without receiving any assistance with their abuse issues, they will continue to suffer not only from social anxiety disorder but may also have post-traumatic stress disorder, depression and/or substance abuse.

Technology

Cell phones, video games, computers, online movies. People who already predisposed to having social anxiety disorder find that technology is an easy way to avoid communicating with others. Hiding behind a device, avoiding conversation, human interaction or even talking on the phone is solved by the use of technology.

The causes f having a social anxiety disorder are many and complex. Most often beginning in childhood, it can be a combination of genetics, upbringing, and environment.

Social anxiety disorder can be learned by children through observation, direct and informational experiences.

The brain structure and chemical imbalances and how the brain is affected when a person is fearful also play a part in the development of SAD.

Being bullied, picked on either by their peers, parents, siblings, family members, or persons in authority, also impacts on how a child can begin to develop a social anxiety disorder.

There are those people who, although may have been bullied or had traumatic experiences happen in their younger years, have social anxiety, but their fears are less pronounced, and it is only specific situations where their fear comes into play.

Their fear may be about speaking before a group or meeting new people, but they get through it and, as they continually expose themselves to the situations they try to avoid, find it to be somewhat easier each time.

Some people with SAD recognize their disorder and seek out help via mental health professionals and learn how to deal with their social phobias.

The next chapter will show how people who have social anxiety disorder learn to deal with their fears of being judged, and their tendency to withdraw from social situations and learn how to be more positive about themselves.

Chapter 3: Social Anxiety Disorder – Techniques and Tips to Deal with It

Most people enjoy getting together at social events, meeting new people, dining out, or participating with their team presenting a new client campaign to upper management. These are situations that are easy and normal for anyone who doesn't have social anxiety.

However, people who live with a social anxiety disorder are not happy that they have this type of disorder. Meeting new people, social events, or even be a participant in a team presentation can cause a wave of anxiousness and fear that can be crippling.

Living with this type of disorder is extremely debilitating, disheartening and can lead to side effects that can only exacerbate the condition. Finding help and relief can offer a positive difference for a person with SAD.

If you are in the throes of social anxiety or know of someone who exhibits the type of symptoms that have been outlined in the previous chapters, this chapter will show what techniques and tips that can be implemented to help deal with SAD.

People with SAD have trouble making friends, finding romantic partners, building a career, even attending family events. However, as difficult as this disorder is, there are treatments that are available to help.

Although there is the treatment approach that combines cognitive-behavioral therapy (CBT) and/or medication, SSRIs, there is self-help that can be implemented to help overcome social anxiety.

Effective self-help plans frequently pull from elements of more established approaches. As an example, a self-help plan may integrate exposure to situations a person fears, the reprogramming of thoughts and different types of relaxation methods.

If you have moderate to mild social anxiety, you may feel that you're not able to move forward and trapped. The only way to move forward and release yourself from this feeling is to begin to work towards doing something positive.

Make an effort to get out into the world – Yes, it's scary and it's much easier to side-step social situations. However, if you suffer from SAD the most important thing you can do for yourself is to get out into the world and begin to live. Go out to places that give you an uncomfortable feeling, accept invitations, and meet new people. (Cuncic, 2019)

While you begin to get out and about, you need to fortify yourself and prepare to handle getting out into the world the right way.

Seek help – Now is the time to seek help. Putting it off to next week is not an option. Frankly, you need to make a commitment to yourself to work towards moving forward and work through this disorder that doesn't serve you well. Don't wait until you're in crisis. The best thing you can do is make an appointment to see someone – today!

You may feel overwhelmed and have that "where do I begin?" mentality. You can seek help and possibly a reference from your physician, but if you're too embarrassed to do that, or don't have a primary care professional to turn to, you can contact the **National Alliance on Mental Illness at** https://www.nami.org to find a mental health professional in your area and who specializes in SAD and phobia disorders. Finding a stranger that is anonymous so you can make the entire process less intimidating and it can possibly lead you to receive help.

Taking the first is the hardest but can be the first of many steps you'll take to distance yourself from this debilitating condition.

Get healthy – Make sure that your health is up to par and that being in poor health is not adding to your anxiety. If you're not in good health, make every effort to improve it.

Do regular exercise routines such as weight training and cardiovascular exercise. Walking even for 20 minutes a day three times a week is a good start. Eat a balanced, healthy diet.

Since your nervous system becomes elevated when you become anxious and stress due to SAD, refrain from drinking caffeinated coffee and sodas, and alcohol. Drink tea, preferably chamomile, to calm your nerves.

If you don't have an exercise plan and are not regularly exercising, begin a program. In order to reduce anxiety and stress and increase positive feelings of well-being, starting an exercise program is a way to achieve this.

Exercising with others can give you the opportunity to practice your social skills in an environment that does not provoke any of the usual fears and is a non-threatening place.

If you don't have the time or resources to make regular exercise classes or join a gym, you can still get your exercising into your day. Taking a walk in your neighborhood or at a nearby park or practicing yoga at home are some options.

You can purchase videos or go to YouTube and find yoga instructors that teach entry level to advance. There are quite a few to choose from. (Cuncic, 2019)

Write your goals down – Writing down your goals down on paper. Read your goals every day. Having unclear, imprecise goals about what you want to achieve will not be enough. Whether you want to become a first-class tennis player or overcome your symptoms of social anxiety, writing down your goals is important. This makes the goals real and perceptible.

Goal setting is where you learn and set benchmarks of where you are now and where and how you decide you want to end up. Find out how you score by taking a self-assessment quiz to measure the level of your social anxiety. That will give you a sense of where you are right now. You can find a number of social anxiety tests that you can take online. Happier Human is a website that has six top quizzes to measure the symptoms of social anxiety. The website is https://www.happierhuman.com/social-anxiety-tests/

Later on, after you've begun to feel that you have a better sense of yourself and what you've been doing to improve your social skills, take the assessment quiz again and see if there's been an improvement in your scores.

Don't compare others success to your own. Compare yourself on how you've been doing a week, a month, or a year ago. That is the most important barometer for you to compare yourself to – yourself and your progress.

Keep a daily journal – In order to see the strides you've made and how you improve over time, keep a daily journal. You'll recognize when you are falling back into negative-thinking and old avoidance habits when you write about your thoughts and experiences.

Since you've written your goals down, you can cross-check and see how you're doing keeping up with them. Jot down some thoughts about your goals and how you've worked towards meeting each one.

Be honest about whether you've been keeping up with them. If not, think about why you haven't and write it down. Before the week is up, go back and read the reasons why you haven't been keeping on track with your goals, then write down what you will be doing about it.

If you're serious about working towards overcoming your social anxiety or at least get a better handle on it, you need to be honest about the work you put into meeting your goals.

Be your own best supporter – Collect information and develop your knowledge about SAD so you may be able to make better decisions. No one is going to look out for you any better than you are. Ask for adjustments at school and work if you think it will be helpful. Don't be afraid to fight for yourself. You need to have positive thoughts because you're taking care of yourself and trying to make improvements. Be your own best cheerleader!

Explain to others, in an educated manner, what your struggles are and what you are doing to deal with them. People whom you attend school with, or work with will have a better understanding of why you are the way you are. (Cuncic, 2019)

If you're attending a party and feel the need to take a time out, then do so. You need to be kind to yourself and acknowledge what you can and cannot handle.

Honor who you are – Realize that there are challenges that you face that are more than others have to. Recognize the accomplishments in your life, no matter how small. There may be days that you will be able to be proud of the fact that you actually left the house.

You may not be a great public speaker, but there are many things in your life that you've accomplished that you can take pride in. Build on those small accomplishments and you'll feel a lot better about yourself.

Social Skills – Practice Them Often

You may have a condition that limits you in speaking with people or in front of a group of them, but there are ways that you can improve on the skills that you do have.

Making introductions – practice doing this by making good eye contact and remembering names. Learn how to give a compliment. If you're making introductions in a business setting and there is hand-shaking all around, practice having a firm (not bone crushing) handshake. It's a universal sign of being assuredness and strength.

If you're interested in improving your public speaking skills, look for a group or organization that encourages public-speaking like Toastmasters International, Public Speaking Courses Online (Udemy), and Public Speaking Courses & Training (LinkedIn Learning).

Whether you choose an online course on Udemy, LinkedIn or Toastmasters International, or join a branch of Toastmasters that you can attend at a branch location, you will benefit from the practice and guided instruction you can receive from them. Some people are born with the gift of gab and others well; they learn how to develop it.

Be assertive – Many people who have SAD also lack assertiveness. The problem is that you don't allow others the opportunity to meet your needs. Assertiveness is being clear about your wants and needs from others so you can be satisfied. It's not to be confused with being aggressive to go after want.

Share experiences – If you've already overcome your social anxiety disorder or are in the midst of working towards conquering your condition, your experiences should be shared because they are valuable and pertain to who you are and what you are going through. (Cuncic, 2019)

You may be surprised that sharing your experiences will help others discover that they are not the only ones who may feel the same way you do or have certain aspects of social anxiety they never realized were affecting them.

Another positive aspect of sharing your experiences is that it will bring awareness to a problem that has been kept in the dark. People don't like to admit they have social anxiety because to others it may seem like a sign of weakness. This is a totally incorrect assumption. It is a mental health condition and has nothing to do with weakness.

It takes a very strong individual to admit to their problems, seek help with them and work at overcoming them. Food for thought.

Begin to say NO– Do you feel as if you're a pushover? Have you had others make demands on you that are unrealistic that they themselves wouldn't perform? Do you have people who treat you badly, but you don't stand up for yourself or to them because you feel incapable of doing so?

Now is the time to begin learning how to say "No" to the unrealistic requests and become more assertive. Clearly, state that you don't want to do what is being asked of you because it's unrealistic.

If you're spoken to disrespectfully and treated badly, let the other person know that it's unacceptable treatment. State it clearly, without stress or anger, but plainly and tell them not to repeat doing so.

If you don't communicate what you want and need clearly, other people can't guess how you feel or what you're thinking.

Begin to say YES – Rather than falling into the same social anxiety pattern of saying "NO" to everything, like an invitation to a social gathering, try saying "YES" for a change. If you receive invitations to social gatherings, try accepting them more often. There may be feelings of anxiousness when you first begin to attend these events, but the more you do, the less stress, anxiety and fear you'll feel.

So, the next time an invitation arrives in your email, or the team at work invites you to join them for lunch when they grab a bite at the local sandwich shop, give it whirl, make the effort and go!

Find a support group – Joining a support group, whether it's a weekly meeting outside of the home or an online group, will help you to find support and camaraderie with others who understand what you are going through. (Cuncic, 2019).

Accept the help the group offers and encourage and help others who struggle as well. You understand what others in the group are going through and offering help to even one other person is an act of kindness that will be paid back to you.

State that you feel nervous – There isn't a person who hasn't felt a bit nervous when they speak in public. One of the best ways to get over the anxiety about public speaking is to actually acknowledge the group or audience that you're nervous before you begin. It breaks the ice and actually, there are more people in that group or audience who have probably felt exactly the same way when they had to speak publicly.

Go somewhere new – Is your routine get up, shower, get dressed, commute to the office, work, eat lunch, work some more (throw in the occasional meeting), finish up your work for the day and go home, eat dinner, catch a TV program or two and go off to bed? How about your weekends? Still, shop at the same grocery store, and eat out at the same restaurant for brunch every Sunday?

It's time to *cut back on the boring* and break up the monotonous routine. Get out and go somewhere new. You may not be able to break up the routine of your work schedule and your commute, but you can break up your weekend routine by going somewhere new.

Try a new restaurant for Sunday brunch and challenge your social anxiety with new surroundings. Discover other sections of your neighborhood that you've been missing. You'll be surprised how a change of scenery can lift up your spirits and help you find a whole new world.

Get a new outfit – Social anxiety can't be cured by retail therapy, but sometimes buying a new outfit can really make you feel upbeat and give you a new attitude.

Purchase something that's different from what you would normally choose to buy. Perhaps, an accessory that complements the outfit and gives it flair. It can be something that will start conversations with others at your job or people who are meeting you for the first time.

Work on building friendships (and keeping them) – Friendships are a great thing to have. Although you've struggled with social anxiety disorder, you may be at a point that you're ready to develop a friendship, maybe even two. It's time to work at getting to know someone better and possibly turning that person into a friend.

It may seem a bit difficult at first, but as time passes it will give you a good feeling to see someone at work or in class who you're familiar with. Take the lead and offer to get together and go out to dinner, take in a movie, or study for the class you both take and grab a bite afterward. Don't wait for the other person to always do the inviting.

Social anxiety disorder can be a difficult condition to overcome, but if your condition is mild or moderate, there are things that you can do to help break yourself free.

Realize that all changes take time and your feelings of fear, stress, and anxiousness will not disappear overnight. But do not feel defeated. If you're willing to work through the rough patches and use some of the techniques and tips suggested in this chapter, you will see the small but steady steps being made and moving forward.

Right now it's important to begin taking hold of this disorder. Don't worry so much about your goals for the time being. Focus on how you're going to get started, seek help, and celebrate the small steps of progress that you will see once you begin your journey using self-help strategies. (Cuncic, 2019)

Chapter 4: Overcoming Social Anxiety Disorder – How to Work through It

People who are dealing with social anxiety disorder often times choose to avoid situations they foresee will cause them to become anxious or stressed. Their fear of being humiliated, meeting new people, even eating in public cause so much discomfort that people with SAD withdraw into themselves.

Social anxiety has been linked to the risk for depression, loneliness, alcohol, drug abuse, the decrease in professional advancement, and the probability of a person never marrying.

However, all is not lost for some of these individuals. There are ways that a person with SAD can do something about improving their condition and working through it to have a healthier way of being and a brighter outlook on life.

There is a drug-free approach made by cognitive behavioral therapists that have made tremendous advances with these problems. As noted in the previous chapter, cognitive behavioral therapy (CBT) has become effective in treating social anxiety disorder. The therapy focuses on your behavior and what you think.

What your thought processes are and what you are thinking plays a large part of someone dealing with social anxiety. This therapy delves into the mind of the sufferer and asks the questions that will give therapists a better idea of how to treat someone with SAD and get the person to recognize what really is the underlying reason that causes them to have this disorder.

What is a person with SAD avoiding – A person with social anxiety tends to side-step situations that provoke anxiety, which is a behavioral problem. When there is the anticipation of going to a social event, like a party, just the idea brings on the feeling of anxiousness. When they decide they won't go because for them it's just too stressful, the decision automatically decreases their anxiety.

The link between the decision to not go to the party and the reduction of their anxiety strengthens their avoiding or escaping having to go to the party altogether. (Leahy Ph.D., 2014)

The reduction of anxiety based on their decision of avoidance reinforces the idea that avoiding what causes their anxiety is the better decision. This automatic decrease in their anxiety leads the person to believe that in order for them to feel less anxious, they should avoid going to parties or other social events.

A major factor of cognitive behavioral therapy is to have the individual with SAD go to social settings and situations and remain in them so that they can learn that nothing is going to happen to them to embarrass or humiliate them and their fears and anxiety will diminish.

The individual also learns that they are able to attend social situations and their readiness to confront their fears can be encouraging. They begin to recognize that they are someone who can actually go to social events and become inspired to do so more often.

One of the first things that can be done to help someone with social anxiety is to have them make a list of all the situations they are avoiding. The list should include how each situation makes them feel since there are varying degrees of anxiety. Some situations arouse more anxiety than others.

Scoring the fear – Identifying how each situation can be given a score in the levels of anxiety that you experience. Your behavior can be scored in terms of the level you might expect. For example, based on a behavior of no anxiety at all to the extreme, panic attack anxiety, no anxiety would be scored at zero while the extreme behavior of a panic attack would be scored as a 10.

The situation of going to a party will be scored by the level of anxiety each segment concerning the party is looked at. Thinking about the party prior to attending would be a 3, going to the party would be a 5, walking into the party and seeing people at the party would be a 6, making an attempt to have a conversation would be an 8. This is how just one situation – attending a party- can be scored.

Writing down how you predict you will feel is important so you can compare how anxious you actually are when you go. In the predicted scoring, some people found that their predictions of how they would feel were higher than what they actually experienced when they attended the party.

Testing the predictions – We frequently forget that we manage better than we think we can handle our anxiety. You can write down what you think about how anxious you believe you'll be for each situation.

What did you predict about your level of anxiety? How long did you remain in that anxious state? These questions will help to test your catastrophe predictions.

For example, making the attempt to have a conversation with a few people at the party was scored as a predicted 8. The person who scored this not only thought the anxiety level would be this high, the also thought they would get tongue-tied and would become so anxious that they would have to leave the party. (Leahy Ph.D., 2014)

What actually happened is they were initially anxious during the beginning of the conversation. But once the conversation began to have a flow and the person became more comfortable, the anxiety level was reduced to a 3. The person did not leave the party and enjoyed the conversation more than they thought they would.

It is a good idea to be clear about what you predict so you can determine whether what you're expecting as a level of anxiety is more than what actually happens. Keep a log about your predictions to compare how anxious you actually become, and whether you begin to improve and see your anxiety levels diminish each time you expose yourself to what you've feared.

Identify and remove safety behaviors – People who have social anxiety take part in behavior that they believe will keep them safe or less likely to humiliate or embarrass themselves.

Some of these "safety" behaviors include using drugs or alcohol to self-medicate themselves, avoiding eye contact, continually wiping their hands to hide that their hands are sweating, rehearsing what they would say, talking very fast, and holding their glass very tightly so people can't see their hands shaking.

The biggest problem with these safety behaviors is that you believe using them are the only way you can shoulder through these experiences by using them each time you're faced with an anxious situation.

Rather than leaning on these behaviors and using them as a safety blanket, giving them up will give you a feeling of having more control and power over your anxiety. You'll be thinking about how you got through situations that would normally provoke your anxiety and did it without rehearsing what you would say or without having a drink to fortify yourself.

Challenge yourself and your negative thoughts – Your predictions of how badly you'll do, how you'll make a fool of yourself and will become embarrassed, how people will notice you're being sweaty, how you trip over your words and that they'll talk about.

You think all these things are catastrophic, but these thoughts can be challenged. Asking yourself whether you actually made yourself look foolish or are you predicting that the same things will happen over and over?

- o Could it be that no one is noticing your hands shaking or your palms sweating because they're thinking about what they're going to say while having the conversation with you?
- o Is there any evidence that your anxiety is what people are talking about? Do you really know what they're talking about?

- Why do you think people care about your anxiety? Does it relate to them in some way?
- Have you ever heard someone else remark that they forgot what they were going to say? Did something bad happen when they said that? (Leahy Ph.D., 2014)

Other negative thoughts and beliefs that add on to the fears and anxiety include:

- Thinking you'll end up looking foolish
- The anxiety and nervousness will come out in your voice and you'll embarrass yourself
- You believe people who are new will probably think you're stupid

An effective way to reduce your symptoms of social anxiety is to challenge these predictive and negative thoughts. Predicting what is going to happen and believing that it's happening while you're in the situation that causes your anxiety may be the reason you set yourself up to feeling the anxiety that you don't need.

Do what makes you anxious – Now that you've identified what makes you anxious in situations and you've scored what affects you from the least to the most anxious, it's time to face your fears.

It helps to imagine each step of the situation and how your anxiety manifests as you think about the example that we've been working on – going to a party. Each step of the situation is what you previously scored;

ranking each step by the level of anxiety you predicted you would feel.

Begin with picturing yourself walking into the party and having the thought that everyone can see that you're anxious. At that moment realize that no one can see your inner feelings. They're focusing on themselves and the other people they may be greeting or may be having conversations with others. They may be thinking about their own concerns and perhaps, their own anxiety. Continue to picture this thought and let go of the anxiety.

You can start practicing what makes you anxious and what you fear. Don't have a drink before you go to the party. Rather, walk into the party, acknowledge that you may have a moment of anxiety and continue to walk in while saying you'll walk in and greet people even if I feel anxious.

Having anxiety at the moment you enter the party is okay. The point of acknowledging it is so you actually learn you can do things while you're feeling anxious and there's no disaster.

It may seem an impossibility to overcome a social situation that provokes your anxiety and fears, but it can be done a step at a time. It begins with a situation that you work your way through to handle and graduate to more challenging situations.

This type of procedure builds your coping skills and your confidence as you make your way to a goal that you set to be less anxious or eradicate your anxiety entirely.

For example, you've become more comfortable and have reduced your anxiety about attending a party. The next step can be that you introduce yourself to at least one new person at each social event.

It may be nerve-wracking and escalate your anxiety in the beginning, but if you employ the lessons you've learned when you took the first steps in going to a party and apply them, you may be surprised how it becomes easier to extend your hand in a greeting to someone new.

Give yourself a reward – People who are socially anxious frequently review themselves and how they performed. They *self-critique* everything they did or said after attending a social situation. This post-social event critique adds to the anxiety of what you think will happen at the next social situation.

Rather than self-critiquing, it would be good to replace it with congratulating yourself for confronting your fears and doing what you had difficulty doing before. You can reward yourself for just going to the party and trying to go through with it even though it was uncomfortable.

Every time you confront your fears, you will win and overcome another portion of your anxiety. (Leahy Ph.D., 2014)

Thought processes that promote social anxiety – You need to consider whether or not you're taking part in unhelpful styles of thought like *personalizing* where you think and assume that people are attentive or focused on you negatively.

Other types of thoughts that are unhelpful are *mind reading* and *fortune telling*.
When your mind read you assume what other people are thinking and they view you in the negative way you view yourself.

Predicting the future, as was noted earlier in the chapter, you assume the worst will happen even before the situation is a reality. You assume that whatever the event is – a party, a business event, or meeting new people – will go terribly. You're feeding into your anxiety even before you're in the reality of the event.

Turn your attention to others, not on yourself – When we're nervous because of a social situation that makes us stress and brings about our anxiety, we tend to get involved in our thoughts about how anxious we are. You may feel that everyone is judging you, and you focus on your body's sensations. In doing this you feel that you will have more control. (Smith M.A., 2019)

However, the extreme self-focus only increases your awareness of how anxious and nervous you are feeling, exacerbating your anxiety. This self-focus distracts you from focusing on the people and conversations around you.

Rather than internalizing and focusing on your anxiety, externalizing and concentrating on others can help in reducing your social anxiety. You can't pay attention to your inner anxiety and the external conversations at the same time. The more you give attention to what's going on around you, the less your anxiety will affect you.

Pay attention to other people by engaging them in conversation and focusing on what they're talking about rather than thinking about what you think they're thinking of you.

Realize that your anxiety isn't that visible. It's only because you are feeling anxious that you believe others can see it. Even if someone does notice you're nervousness, it doesn't mean they're judging you or thinking of you negatively. It may be that the person who recognizes your nervousness *is because they've felt that way as well.*

Listen to what the other person is saying and **be in the moment**. Don't worry about what you're going to say or focus on any mistake you may think you've made and resist from listening to the negative thoughts in your head. Stop beating yourself up. (Smith M.A., 2019)

Control your breathing – your body goes through many changes when you are anxious. Your breathing is quicker and if you are having extreme anxiety you may hyperventilate and become dizzy, your heart rate increases and have a feeling of suffocating.

Slowing your breathing can help bring your physical symptoms under control.
Practice breathing techniques by:

- o Sitting in a comfortable position
- o Slowly inhaling through the nose for four seconds
- o Hold your breath for two seconds
- o Slowly exhale through your mouth for six seconds and push out as much air as possible

Continue the process for a few minutes as practice. The practice will come in handy when you feel anxious and want to calm yourself and bring your breathing back to normal.

The process to work through social anxiety takes time and patience. The techniques that can be used to begin the process of managing your anxiety need to be applied almost daily in the beginning. However, over time and with practice, you may begin to see a difference in your attitudes and a diminishing of the fears you had in the beginning.

Facing your fear of social situations is a systematic, gradual process. It's better to face them than to avoid them.

You may benefit from additional guidance and support from a therapist if you are attempting to use the self-help practices and exercises on your own and run into any roadblocks.

CBT techniques, social skills training, and role-playing are frequently used as part of a therapy group. You will become more comfortable and find your anxiety will diminish as you practice and prepare for situations that you fear. (Smith M.A., 2019)

Chapter 5: How to Deal with Anxiety

Anxiety is having the feelings of fear, worry, and nervousness and felt on the mental, physical, and emotional levels.

Experiencing anxious feelings is not uncommon for almost everyone. For example, a person can become anxious because they want to get tickets for what could be the last Rolling Stones concert and are hoping that they get the seats they want. This is not a situation that raises fear or is negative in nature, but there is some worry that is linked to the anxious feelings.

Another example is a bride before her wedding. She becomes anxious about *everything*. The date, the venue, the dress, her weight, her hair, her bridesmaids, the rings, the guest list and seating, the food and cake for the reception, the flowers, and the list goes on. This anxiety is a bit different and there is fear and worry involved because the bride wants everything to be perfect and is afraid there will be a glitch that may come up and get in the way of her perfect wedding day vision.

Then there is the anxiety that is experienced and is extreme. On a cognitive level, a person may have disturbing thoughts. Emotionally, they feel scared and on the physical level. It can manifest in shortness of breath, shaking, and breaking out in a sweat.

The most extreme anxiety is the common symptoms of people with social anxiety disorder. People who suffer from panic disorder are aware of the struggle of managing their feelings anxious and that it is taking over or spiraling out of their control.

Anxiety Toll

Your body knows when anxiety is taking its toll. You have a problem eating, concentrating and sleeping. You get an upset stomach, headaches and in the middle of all of the things affecting you physically, you may even suffer a panic attack, feeling dizzy while your heart pounds against your chest.

Anxiety may also have the earmarks of depression. Anxiety and depression sometimes intersect.

When our anxiety interferes with daily activities that it prevents you from going out and enjoying life but instead becomes so overwhelming, it is time to get some help.

When you feel like you have a continuous worry loop going on in your head, you may have Generalized Anxiety Disorder (GAD). It's like having a worry machine going on and on, all day, every day. (WebMD, 2009)

You procrastinate to a point where you resist taking a step. You become nervous about going to a party that you responded you would attend, and you decide at the last minute that you won't go. The anxiety problem may be more serious than you realize.

How does one manage – Manage the things you can and accept those you can't change. You need to ask yourself where you can make changes, where you can take control and then do what has to be done.

Quite often the help of family and friends – anyone who you are close with and who you feel you can trust and won't judge (very important) – can help you get past a cycle of anxiety. However, if you are overwhelmed and feel no relief in changes you make and the effort you put into turning things around on your own, it is time to meet with a therapist or possibly be prescribed with medication.

Does anxiety overwhelm you? There are steps that you can take to help manage the anxiety.

Breathe – When your heartbeat begins to feel like it's going to come out of your chest, beating faster and harder in response to a situation that is stressful, or you begin to feel damp in your clothing, or you feel your palms getting sweaty when you're challenged with a task or event that's overwhelming – those are the feelings of anxiety and our body's responding to the stress that accompanies it.

Giving a presentation in front of a large group, your first day at a new job, or going on your first date are triggers that bring on anxiety. We all have different triggers and recognizing them is one of the most significant steps to managing your anxiety.

Recognizing your triggers takes self-reflection and time. While you are learning what your triggers are, there are things you can adapt to try helping yourself keep calm and prevent your anxiety from taking over. (Hirschlag, 2018)

Homeopathic remedies - If you have intermittent anxiety that gets in the way of your being able to focus or complete your tasks, there are homeopathic remedies that can assist in taking control of the situation that is causing you anxiety.

Your anxiety may be focused and involve an event that is quickly approaching. However, your anxiety is brief and subsides after the event actually takes place.

Examine your thought patterns – Your mind may have negative thoughts and garble the harshness of the situation. Questioning if the thoughts are true is one way to confront your fears and see where you can regain control.

Walk – There are times to put a stop to thoughts that are elevating your anxiety is to walk. Walk away from the situation, walk and breathe in the fresh air, walk and take in your surroundings. You will walk your anxiety away when you focus on your walk.

Jot your thoughts down – What is it that's making you anxious? When you jot it down, it's now in black and white on paper and no longer swirling around in your mind.

Aromatherapy – Scents of chamomile, sandalwood, and lavender in incense, a candle or oil can be extremely soothing. The fragrances and their aroma are thought to activate the brain and possibly ease anxiety

These tips for relaxation are very helpful for those who intermittently become anxious. The tips may also be used by someone with generalized anxiety order (GAD) when they need to take control of their anxiety.

However, speedy methods to manage anxiety aren't the only treatments to use if you have GAD. There are long-term approaches to help reduce the harshness of the symptoms and even inhibit them from happening.

Long-Term Approaches for Managing Anxiety

If anxiety is part of your life occurring on a regular basis, it's imperative to discover treatment plans to help to keep the anxiousness and anxiety in check. It could be a mix of mediation and talk therapy or removing or resolving a trigger that escalates the anxiety.

If there are questions you need to be answered and are not sure where to begin in finding treatments, talk with a mental health professional. They may be able to guide you and suggest treatments and strategies you had not thought of before.
 (Hirschlag, 2018)

Recognize and Control Your Triggers

Recognize your triggers with the assistance of a therapist or on your own. Some of the triggers are apparent – alcohol, drugs, caffeine or smoking. Frequently they are not as obvious.

Problems that are long-term, such as work-related issues, or financial worries may take longer to pinpoint. Is it a person, due date or the situation? You may need additional support either with friends or through therapy.

When you do pinpoint your trigger, limit your exposure to it as much as you can. If it's not possible to put a cap on it like if the trigger is due to working in a stressful situation that is not possible to change at the moment, using other managing techniques may help.

General triggers

- o Stressful work environment or job
- o Commuting to work
- o Genetics
- o Caffeine
- o Chronic pain

- o Illnesses that are chronic such as asthma, diabetes or heart disease
- o Drug withdrawal
- o Withdrawal or side effects of particular medications
- o Phobias such as claustrophobia, fear of small spaces, or agoraphobia, fear of open or crowded spaces
- o Trauma
- o Possible other mental illness like depression

Cognitive behavioral therapy (CBT) – People learn different ways they react to situations that cause anxiety. Changing negative behaviors and thought patterns before they get out of control can be helped by consulting a therapist to develop strategies.

Meditation – Originating from Buddhist teachings, mindfulness meditation is the most well-liked meditation technique.

You pay attention to your thoughts while they are in your mind. You don't become involved or judge the thoughts. You take note of patterns.

This type of meditation helps you to concentrate on awareness and when practiced on a regular basis can help train the brain to diminish anxious thoughts as they occur. (Hirschlag, 2018)

Change your diet or take supplements
– Taking supplements or changing your diet is a long-term plan. Research has shown that particular nutrients or supplements help in reducing anxiety.

The supplements suggested are:

- o Lemon balm
- o Ashwagandha
- o Valerian root
- o Green tea
- o Omega-3 fatty acids
- o Kava kava
- o Dark chocolate – in moderation

In order for your body to be running on the nutritional herbs and foods that your body receives; it can take approximately three months to begin to feel and see results. Consult your physician to talk about the herbal supplements if you're taking other medications.

Keep healthy – Regular exercise, getting enough sleep, having a balanced diet and remaining connected with people who care about you are good ways to avert anxiety symptoms.

Taking medications – If your mental health professional recommends that you would benefit from medication because your anxiety is severe, there are a number of avenues to go, depending on our symptoms. Consult your doctor to discuss your concerns.

When is my anxiety damaging – It can be a challenge recognizing what type of anxiety you're dealing with because a person's perceived danger, compared to another person, can be totally different.

You've probably heard the term anxiety as an overall term for feeling nervous, uneasy or worried. It's frequently a feeling that responds to an uncertain outcome to an upcoming event.

It's part of our brain's reaction to perceived danger, even if the danger isn't actually real. Everyone deals with anxiety at some time or another in their life.

However, anxiety can become more serious. There are times that it can turn into anxiety attacks. These attacks feel manageable in the beginning and then progressively build over a short time.

Anxiety attacks are not to be confused with panic attacks. A panic attack strikes immediately and then eases off. (Hirschlag, 2018)

Symptoms of an anxiety attack - These are some of the common physical and mental symptoms of anxiety:

- o Nervousness or agitation
- o Rapid heart rate
- o Feelings of dread, panic or danger
- o Chills or trembling
- o Weakness
- o Stomach problems
- o Hyperventilation
- o Distraction and difficulty focusing

The managing strategies for anxiety may also help to control a panic attack. It is possible to have a panic and anxiety attack at the same time.

Focusing on an object, closing your eyes, or repeating a mantra are strategies to manage panic attacks:

- Palpitating heart
- Shortness of breath
- Feeling you're losing control
- Afraid of dying
- Chest pains
- Feeling dizzy or lightheaded
- Nausea
- Feelings of hot or cold
- Extremities tingling or numb

The Reasons and Causes of Anxiety

You may follow and use these tips and notice they haven't been working. If so, you may give some thought to seeking help from a professional particularly if you believe you have GAD and if it's inhibiting your ability to get on with routine activities and if you're experiencing physical symptoms.

You can recognize your triggers and manage long-term plans through medication, behavior therapy, and more with a mental health professional assisting in simplifying the process.

Anxiety should not control your day-to-day activities. It may always be a part of your life, but even the most excessive anxiety disorders can be treated so your symptoms aren't so overwhelming.

Medication

Anxiety disorders will not be cured by medication, but it will help you to keep it under control. There are a few options if anxiety becomes severe enough.

Many types of anxiety disorders are being treated by antidepressants, in particular, SSRIs. SSRIs have been prescribed in conjunction with Xanax, Valium, and Ativan.

These drugs have side effects that include poor concentration, irritability, and drowsiness and can be addictive when using them long-term.

Certain anxiety disorders, particularly social anxiety disorder have had Beta-blockers prevent physical symptoms.

Chapter 6: How to Stop Anxiety Using Calming and Relaxing Techniques

Anxiety and stress can create an imbalance in our nervous system. Our routine of work, family, and responsibilities on a daily basis can deplete our energy and make us even more susceptible to moments of anxiety and stress.

With a nervous system running overtime, it's no wonder that our nerves are frayed, our patience is tried, and our moments of irritation are not, shall we say our most shining moments.

We may believe that when we get home and finally have time to relax and chill out that parking ourselves in front of the TV and zoning out will reduce our stress. However, this does very little to reduce the effects of our stress.

To combat stress effectively, the body's natural relaxation response needs to be activated. This can be achieved by practicing calming and relaxation techniques such as meditation, deep breathing, yoga, and exercise.

Find time to fit in these types of activities as they can help increase your energy and make your mood upbeat, diminish stress and improve physical and mental health.

Relaxation Response

Your body overflows with chemicals when stress overwhelms and overtakes your nervous system. When you need to act quickly, these chemicals prepare you for "fight or flight." In an emergency, these stress responses can save your life in case of an emergency situation. But when the stresses of everyday life constantly activate these chemicals it can take its toll on your physical and emotional health and wear your body down.

Although no one can avoid stress all the time, you can counteract its damaging effects. Learn to generate a state of deep rest known as the *relaxation response*. This is the opposite of the stress response. Your body and mind are brought back into a state of balance with the relaxation response.

When activated, the relaxation response will:

- Bring the heart rate down
- Breathing is deeper and slower
- Stabilizes or decreases blood pressure
- Relaxes the muscles
- Increases blood flow to the brain

Additionally, the relaxation response increases focus and energy, fights against, illness, lessens aches and pains, increases problem-solving abilities, and improves motivation and productivity along with its calming physical effects.

What's really beneficial about relaxation response is anyone can realize these benefits if they practice regularly. Most relaxation techniques are available with free audio downloads, or inexpensive apps easily downloaded to a smartphone if you choose not to pay for professional acupuncture or massage sessions.

Realize that you need to practice a relaxation technique rather than just watching TV or lying on the couch or reading. Although sometimes relaxing, the mind and body do not get enough of the psychological and physical benefits of the relaxation response.

Look for the methods of relaxation that is best for you

Everyone is different when it comes to finding a relaxation method that is right for them. The method that is the right one for you is the one that makes you feel comfortable, is able to interrupt your everyday thoughts and focus your mind to provoke the relaxation response and fits into your lifestyle.

How you respond to stress may also affect the relaxation method that works the best. You may find that combining different methods or alternating different methods gives the best results.

Different Relaxation Techniques

Immobilization response – Experiencing trauma of some type and having a tendency to become stuck or freeze under stress, you need to rouse your nervous system to "fight or flight" response so you can practice the stress relief techniques. To accomplish this, select a physical activity that has both your arms and legs, such as dancing, tai chi or running and do the exercise mindfully by concentrating on the feeling in your legs as you move.

Fight response – You will respond best to activities that promote stress relief that calms you down such as progressive muscle relaxation, guided imagery, deep breathing or meditation.

Flight response – You will respond best to activities that relieve stress, energize the nervous system, and are stimulating. Practice massage, rhythmic exercise, mindfulness, or power yoga if you are prone to becoming withdrawn, depressed or dazed when you're under stress. (Robinson L. S., 2019)

Do you like social stimulus or time alone?

If you enjoy and hanker for social communication, you will probably like a class setting that will give you support and stimulation and may help keep you motivated.

However, if you like to do things on your own and crave solitude, meditation, or progressive muscle relaxation are solo techniques that will help revitalize the batteries and calm the mind.

Deep breathing - Deep breathing is easy to learn, you can practice techniques anywhere, gives you a quick way to reduce your stress levels and, with the focus on full, purgative breaths, it is a powerful yet simple relaxation technique.

The cornerstone of many other practices of relaxation, deep breathing can be combined with other elements of relaxation such as music and aromatherapy. There are apps and downloads that can lead you through the process. All that's needed is a place to stretch out and a few minutes to practice the technique.

Practice deep breathing – Breathe deeply from your abdomen, not from your chest. Breathing from the abdomen activates the nerve that runs down the neck and through the chest and colon and is known as the *vagus nerve*. Activating this nerve stimulates your relaxation response which diminishes the blood pressure and heart rate and lowers stress levels.

In order to practice breathing properly, you need to position yourself sitting up comfortably in order to execute the proper breathing technique from the abdomen.

○ Sit with your back straight and supported. Put one hand on your abdomen and the other hand on your chest

- o Inhale and breathe in through the nose. The hand on your chest should have very little movement while the hand on the abdomen should rise.

- o Exhale through your mouth, releasing as much air as possible which contracting your abdominal muscles. The hand on your abdomen should move in as you exhale, while the hand on your chest should have very little movement.

- o Continue to breathe in this manner – inhaling through your nose and exhaling through your mouth. Pay attention to inhale so that your abdomen rises and falls. (Robinson L. S., 2019)

Lay down on the floor if you find that you have difficulty breathing from your abdomen when you're sitting up. Place a small book on your abdomen so that you can see it rise and fall on your abdomen.

Progressive muscle relaxation – Progressive muscle relaxation is when you methodically tense and relax different muscle group in the body and is a two-step process. The method gives you an intimate familiarity with the sensations of tension, as well as the relaxation, that feels like in the different parts of the body when you practice regularly. Your mind relaxes along with the body.

You can combine progressive muscle relaxation with the deep breathing technique to stimulate additional stress relief.

Practice progressive muscle relaxation
Before you begin to practice this relaxation method, consult with your physician in the event that you have a history of back problems or muscle spasms or any other injuries that are serious enough to be irritated by the muscle tensing.

Begin with your feet and work your way up to your body to your face. Tense the muscles intended

- o Get comfortable, take your shoes off, loosen your clothing
- o Inhale and exhale slowly, taking deep breaths for a few minutes

o Begin to pay attention to your right foot and concentrate on how it feels

o Tense the muscles in your right foot slowly, squeezing the foot and toes as tightly as possible. Hold the squeeze for a 10 count

o Relax the foot. Notice on how the tension flows away as you relax the foot letting it feel loose and limp

o Remain in the relaxed state for a moment and breathe, slowly and deeply.

o Turn your attention to the left foot. Follow the same progression of muscle tensing and releasing the foot.

o Slowly move up through the body tightening and relaxing the different muscle groups

In the beginning, it may take some practice to tense only the muscles of the group you are intent in tensing and relaxing. However, over time with regular practice, you'll become proficient and get the full benefit of this relaxation technique.

Sequence of Progressive Muscle Relaxation

- Feet – right foot followed by the left foot
- Calves – right calf followed by the left calf
- Thighs – right thigh followed by the left thigh
- Hips and buttocks
- Abdominal area
- Chest
- Back

- Right hand and arm followed by left hand and arm
- Neck and shoulders
- Face

Meditation – Body Scan Meditation

This meditation type is one that concentrates on numerous parts of the body. The similarity to progressive muscle relaxation is that you begin at your feet and work your way up the body.

However, you will focus on the way each part of your body feels without classifying each part good or bad. There is no tensing of any parts of the body and you will perform this meditation lying down.

Lay on the floor on your back, legs extended and arms at your sides. Relax. You can have your eyes open or closed, whatever is your preference.

Breathe slowly, inhaling in and exhaling out in a measured fashion.

Focus on the toes of your right foot. Notice any sensations you may feel in the toes. Continue to breathe, each deep breath flowing towards your toes. Remain focused on the toes for about two minutes.

Now focus on the sole of your right foot. Take notice of any sensations you may feel in your sole. Envision each breath flowing from the sole to your foot. Continue for one to two minutes.

Move your attention to your right ankle and repeat the process. Move up to the calf, knee, thigh, and hip.

Repeat each process with the left toes, foot, sole, and ankle.

Travel up to the torso, the abdomen and through the lower back, upper back and chest, and shoulders.

Make note of any part of your body that is causing you discomfort or any pain.

Once the body scan is completed, remain on the floor and relax. Remain still and silence, your attention on how your body feels.

Slowly sit up, open your eyes and stretch.

The body will feel refreshed as well as the mind.

Mindfulness Meditation

This is an interesting meditation because it focuses totally on your thoughts and what is happening right now, at the moment, rather than worrying about what's going to happen in the future or dwelling on the past.

Meditations have been used to reduce anxiety, stress, depression and other negative thoughts and emotions and cultivate mindfulness instead. Some of the meditations by having you focus on a single mantra/word or your breathing.

Other mindfulness meditation forms have you follow then release your internal sensations or thoughts. This type of meditation can be practiced while exercising, eating or walking. (Robinson L. S., 2019)

Practicing a Basic Mindfulness Meditation

- o Settle in a quiet place where there will be no distractions or interruptions
- o Sit on the floor with legs crossed or in a straight-backed chair
- o Choose a point to focus on. This can be your breathing or an external focus such as a mantra or a candle's flame.
- o While you are meditating, remain in the now. If other thoughts crop up, don't fight them, but turn your attention away from them and back to the focal point.

Mindful and Rhythmic Exercise

You may not be too high on exercising and it may not sound that soothing, but there are exercises that can be relaxing and can get you into a flow of repetitive movement. (Robinson L. S., 2019)

These exercises are:

- o Running
- o Swimming
- o Walking
- o Dancing
- o Climbing
- o Rowing

In order to maximize relieving your stress, you can always include mindfulness to the workout. You will derive a great benefit from adding a mindfulness element while performing any of these rhythmic exercises. It will help to relieve any anxiety, stress or other negative emotional feelings.

Remember that, just like meditation, mindful exercise is practicing and focusing at the moment. You want to pay attention to the now, focusing on the sensations that you feel in your body and your breathing. If your mind wanders, gently direct it back to what your focal point is, like the movement of your arms and legs while swimming, running or dancing as an example.

Visualization/Guided imagery

This is a bit different variation on conventional meditation where imagery – imagining a scene where you feel peaceful and free to release all anxiety and tension.

This imagery can be whatever you choose – a favorite park, tropical beach, or a quiet place in the woods.

The practice of visualization can be practiced with a therapist or on your own, leading you through the imagery. You can practice visualization with or without audio enhancement such as soothing music or sounds from the sea, rain, or wind in the trees. Match the audio to your imagery such as sounds from the sea should match your tropical beach imagery.

Practice Visualization

Imagine the place you want to envision during your meditation. Close your eyes and focus on visualizing your place as vibrantly and colorfully as possible, seeing, smelling, tasting and feeling your image. You want to visualize your place, not just look at it as a photograph if you incorporate as many physical and sensory specifics as possible. (Robinson L. S., 2019)

For example, if you are thinking of a quiet wooded glen, you want to be:

- o **Hearing** the sound of the breeze in the trees
- o **Seeing** the sun shooting its rays of light through the trees
- o **Feeling** the warmth of the sun on your head, face and body
- o **Smelling** the flowers that cover the forest floor
- o **Tasting** the air that's fresh and clean

The anxiety, stress, and worry will fade away as you explore the place you visualize if you lose track of where you are during visualization because this is normal. Your body may also feel heavy in your legs, as well as your muscles twitching. These responses are normal.

Tai Chi

Tai chi is a non-competitive series of flowing body movements performed slowly. You can practice Tai chi at your own pace. In practicing Tai chi you focus on the movements and breathing, your attention is in the present. Tai chi clears the mind and leads you to a relaxed state.

Tai chi is a low-impact safe choice for people of all fitness levels and ages, including seniors. Like yoga, learning it in a class or private instructor can be a benefit. When you've learned the basic principles of the movements you can practice at home, or with others.

Tai chi is a safe, low-impact option for people of all ages and fitness levels, including older adults and those recovering from injuries. As with yoga, it's best learned in a class or from a private instructor. Once you've learned the basics, you can practice alone or with others.

Yoga

Yoga works very well in reducing anxiety and stress. A practice of both stationary and moving poses and blending together with deep breathing, it also improves strength, flexibility, stamina, and balance.

Learning yoga with a qualified instructor either in a class, with a private instructor or by using video instructions to guide you will lessen the possibility of injury if yoga is practiced incorrectly. Once you learn the basic moves and feel comfortable with them, you can practice alone or with others. (Robinson L. S., 2019)

Best Yoga practices for stress

Yoga classes that have steady, slow movements, gentle stretching and deep breathing work best for stress relief

Satyananda – promotes deep relaxation, features gentle poses and meditation. It is suitable for beginners as well as anyone who is looking to reduce their stress

Hatha yoga – is a gentle yoga that relieves stress and also suitable for beginners.

Power yoga -yoga with poses that are intense and concentrates on fitness. This yoga is suited for those who are looking for relaxation and stimulation.

Not sure which yoga class is right for you to relieve your anxiety and stress? Call a yoga studio in your area or ask your teacher.

Self-massage

A massage can help ease muscle tension (those tight shoulders), relieve pain and help reduce stress. Having a professional massage at a health club or a spa can be a wonderful experience if you've never had one, but you can enjoy the same experience at home or work by self-massaging or trading a massage with a loved one.

You can self-massage yourself in bed to unwind and relieve all the stress of the day before you go to bed, on the couch after your day has ended, or at your desk to relieve any stress or muscle tension you may have.

Relieve stress with a self-massage

Use gentle chops with the edge of your hand. For muscle tension, use a combination of strokes. Use your fingertip and put pressure on muscle knots. Try long, light gliding strokes and knead across your muscles.

Apply these strokes to any part of the body that can be within your reach.

To focus a massage on your head and neck:

- o Begin to knead the muscles at the back of the shoulders and neck with a loose fist and drum them up and down the back and sides of your neck.

o Make circles around the base of your skill using your thumbs. Slowly massage your scalp with your fingertips. Don't forget to massage your forehead, temples and jaw muscles.

o Using your middle fingers, massage the bridge of your nose. Massage out over your eyebrows to the temples.

A regular relaxation practice

It takes regular practice to truly feel the effects of these stress-reliever techniques. Learning the basics isn't hard, but they need time and attention to master and incorporate them into your schedule and lifestyle.

It's recommended to set aside at least 10 to 20 minutes a day to practice these relaxation techniques. If you feel you want to have more time to get the maximum benefit from the techniques, especially on days where the anxiety and stress levels are higher, extend your relaxation period to 30 minutes.

- o Set aside time during the day and practice at least once a day.
- o Make use of your smartphone apps
- o Don't practice when you're fighting sleep. You want to execute your techniques to derive their benefits.
- o Don't expect to be an expert during your first few days. Sometimes it can take time to begin to receive the benefits from the effort you've put in.

Don't get discouraged, just begin again and before you know it, you'll be enjoying all the benefits of relieving anxiety and stress and gaining relaxation.

Chapter 7: How to Stop Worrying – Tips and Tricks to Use

Worry. The word is derived from the Olde English word "wyrgan" which originally meant strangle. The definition changed to then mean "harass" and then "cause anxiety to".

Worrying can, in some ways, strangle people, cause anxiety, and harass their thoughts and attitudes as well.

Frankly, worry is a normal part of life. We worry about large and small things. If you take mass transit to commute to work, you worry if your train or bus is running behind schedule, making you late for work. We worry about a job interview, an unpaid bill, an upcoming final exam.

We worry about our kid's safety, their health, or their academic achievement. Whether they're getting enough fresh air and if they're too stuck on video games and Instagram.

What is too much worry? - There's always the worry about what happens in situations every day. However, consistently worrying, always expecting the worst outcome, and negative thinking can be debilitating and take a toll on your physical and emotional health.

Emotionally, it can drain your emotional strength and have you feeling jumpy, tense, distracted, and irritable. Physically, you can end up with headaches, abdominal stress, muscle tension, and a problem sleeping or insomnia. Your concentration at work or school will be taxed.

You may lash out at the people who are closest to you, have negative thoughts and self-medicate with drugs, alcohol, or both.

Generalized Anxiety Disorder (GAD) is a major symptom of chronic worrying and is an anxiety disorder that brings on nervousness, tension, and an overall feeling of unease.

If you are a chronic worrier, there are ways that can help to turn off or at least reduce anxious thoughts. The mental habit of chronic worrying is one that can be broken. It involves training your brain to remain calm and have a vision of life from a less fearful and more balanced outlook.

Why is it difficult to stop worrying? – Worrying constantly keeps you up at night, leaving you tense and irritable during the day. Chronic worriers have beliefs that are both positive and negative and are driven by anxious thoughts.

Beliefs About Worrying

Negative beliefs – You may possibly believe that constant worrying is harmful and is going to affect your physical health. You may also worry that you're losing control about your worrying. Now you're worried about your worrying.

This worrying only adds to the anxiety that builds up and promotes the worrying to continue. Negative beliefs are damaging, but positive beliefs are just as damaging.

Positive beliefs – You may possibly believe that if you worry you can prevent problems, prepare for the worst-case scenario, side-step anything bad that can happen or gives solutions to problems. You may think that maybe if there's a problem and you worry about it enough that you will eventually resolve it. Or maybe you think that the responsible thing to do is to worry to make sure you don't miss anything connected to the problem. (Robinson, 2019)

Tips to Stop Worrying

Worrying over a prolonged period of time can interfere with your daily tasks and activities. It can distract you from school, work or your family. If you develop a way to put off worrying, this can be a help. Instead of chastising yourself and trying to stop worrying, give yourself a set time that will allow you permission to worry. After that set time, you can postpone the worry until later.

Develop a worry period – Set a time and place for you to worry. The time and setting should be the same each day. Choose somewhere in the house where you won't be disturbed and a time that is not close to your bedtime. For example, you'll worry in the family room each day between 4:30 to 4:50 pm.

While you are in your worry period, you can worry about whatever you've been thinking about. Worried about your family, finances, health issues? Whatever has been on your mind you are allowed to worry about. This is your set time. Once you're done, the remainder of the day until your next worry period is to be worry-free.

It may be difficult in the beginning to contain your worry to a twenty-minute time frame, but in time you will be telling yourself that you'll worry about it later when you're in your worry period.

Jot down your worries – Once you have set up your worry period, it doesn't mean that a worry or anxious concern won't cross your mind during the time you supposed to be worry-free. Jot down what you consider a concern and continue getting through the day. You know that you'll be able to worry about it later.

 (Robinson, 2019)

When you write down what's on your mind, it takes a bit more time than just thinking about it, so that concern that you have right now may lose some of its importance once you see it in writing.

Review your worries during your worry period – If you've been jotting down your worries and concerns and they continue to bother you, take the time to worry about them, but only during the time you've set as your worry period.

You'll gain a better and more balanced viewpoint reviewing your worries in this way. Also, if there's a worry that is no longer important, cross it off your worry list and end your worry period for the day.

Challenge Your Anxiety and Thoughts

You may have a viewpoint of the world that makes it seem more menacing than it actually is if you suffer from chronic worry and anxiety. For example, you may treat thoughts that are based on your anxiety as fact when in reality it is the anxiety that you're paying attention to. Or you may predict that a situation will turn out worse than it really does in the end. This is unnecessary energy and anxious feelings poured into a situation that actually turns out better than expected.

This type of thinking is known as cognitive distortions. These types of thoughts include:

Thinking all-or-nothing - Looking at situations as black or white extremes with no middle ground or gray area (the color gray which would be the color of black and white combined). If there isn't total perfection, then you consider yourself a failure.

Overgeneralizing – If you didn't get hired for one job, your thoughts are that you'll *never* get hired for any job again. This is known as overgeneralizing your thoughts based on one experience.

This type of thinking is negative and, in line with the job example, can make you feel defeated even before you search for another job or get called for an interview.

Concentration on negatives and sifting out the positive – Rather than focusing on the positive factors of a situation, you focus on the one factor that is negative.

Discrediting positive events – You may have done extremely well getting a passing grade on a test, but pass it off as being "just lucky" rather than giving yourself credit for putting the study time in to pass the test. (Robinson, 2019)

The worst-case syndrome – Your thoughts immediately jump to the worst-case scenario in a situation. The power goes out temporarily in your office building and but you immediately think that it is a city-wide blackout.

Negative "mind reader" and "fortune telling" thoughts – You're a mind reader when you have thoughts of someone not liking you although you have no evidence of it. The other person has not said or done anything to give you those thoughts, yet you have negative thoughts about the person.

Your thoughts are you *know* something really bad is going to happen. However, there is no evidence that anything is amiss that would lead anyone else to think it.

Making rules for your self-behavior – Making up a list of strict rules of things you should and should not do and berating yourself for breaking any of them. For example, you think you'll only spend an hour at the mall to pick up a specific item and spend two additional hours instead of window shopping. You think you have no integrity in breaking your own rule.

Negative self-thoughts – These thoughts are based on what *you* perceive to be true and not what other people may or may not be thinking. You may feel you're boring, or a failure based on your own negative self-thinking.

Taking responsibility for things not in your control – You assume the blame for something that you have no control over. For example, your daughter is in a rush to go meet friends for a night out and forgets her wallet on her dresser. You think if you hadn't been talking to her before she left, she would have remembered to put it in her bag.

People are normally forgetful. Her wallet not making it into her bag had nothing to do with you speaking with her. She just forgot. (Robinson, 2019)

What You Can Do to Challenge These Thoughts

Challenge the negative thoughts during your worry period. Ask yourself some questions:

- o What proof is there for me to believe what I've thought is true? That it's not true?
- o Can I look at a situation in a more realistic, positive way?
- o Is what I'm fearful of will actually happen? What is the probability of that happening? If the probability is low, what could the more likely outcome be?
- o How will worrying about a situation help me or hurt me?
- o If a friend of mine had this worry, what would I say to them?

Differentiate Between Worries that Can be Solved vs. Those that Can't

Research has shown that when you're in the process of worrying, your anxiety levels are diminished. When you review problems, your thoughts are distracted by your emotions. This gives you a sense of accomplishment. However, worrying and solving any problems are very dissimilar.

When you evaluate a situation, developing specific steps for dealing with it and then implementing the plan and putting it into action is problem-solving. Conversely, just worrying about a situation never leads to a solution.

Regardless of how much time you dwell on worst-case scenarios, it doesn't make you any more equipped to deal with them should they actually happen.

Can your worry solve the problem? – You can take action with solvable, productive worries. For example, if you've been worrying about bills, you have the ability to call your creditors to ask if a payment plan is an option to make the payments easier.

Worries that are unsolvable and not productive are ones to which there is no solution. Prediction questions such as is someone in your family going to get into an accident, or will you be getting the flu this winter are not actionable. There is no answer to those worries.

Start taking action if the worry is solvable – List all the solutions you can think of and focus on the things you have the ability to change instead of realities or conditions that are beyond your control. Once you assess your options, develop a plan and then take action. Having a plan and beginning to do something about the situation, your anxiety will be reduced.

Accept the improbability if your worry is not solvable – The majority of people who are chronic worriers usually fall into this category. Predicting what the future will bring is frequently what the worry is about and is how a person thinks the worry can prevent any surprises that are unpleasant and how the outcome can be controlled.

The truth is, it doesn't work. Worrying about all the worst-case scenarios don't make life any more predictable. Concentrating on these scenarios will take away and distract from appreciating all the things that we have that are good. It's all about being *in the moment* and enjoying the present.

Attempt your need to have immediate answers and the feeling of certainty to stop worrying:

Talk to your family and friends and ask how they manage situations that present uncertainty. Is it possible for you to do the same? (Robinson, 2019)

When you worry about situations that have uncertainty the reason is frequently a way to side-step emotions that are unpleasant. You can begin to be accepting of your feeling, even the ones that don't make sense or make you feel uncomfortable.

Because situations can have uncertainty, do you project that bad things will happen? How likely will something actually happen? If the likelihood is low, can you live with the small possibility that something may happen?

Pause Your Worry Cycle

When you worry extensively, it may seem as if the thoughts running through your mind are constantly negative and are an endless repetitive loop. This probably makes you feel as if you're mind is out of control or you feel like you're burning out from the anxiety and the worry.

There are steps that can be taken to pause all the anxious thoughts and take time away from continuous worrying.

Get moving – Get some exercise. It's a good and effective way to treat anxiety. The body releases endorphins that can relieve stress and tension, increase your energy and improve your well-being.

Another important aspect of exercising is focusing on how your body moves and feels disrupt the consistent stream of worries that run through your mind. Paying attention to your movements, the sound of your feet on the ground and the feeling of the warmth of the sun on your face will help you to feel calmer and have a better state of mind.

Sign up for tai chi or yoga – These are two other ways of having your mind focused on your movements and breathing. You're in the moment, clearing your thoughts and getting relaxed.

If you don't have the time or resources to get to a class, there are excellent DVDs that you can purchase. Also, YouTube has quite a number of videos for both practices that you can review and find one that you feel comfortable with.

Practice deep breathing – If you feel yourself becoming anxious and your worry antennae are up, practice deep breathing exercises that will help to quiet your mind and reduce negative thoughts.

Meditation – Focus on the present and don't worry about the future with meditation. When you are involved in the present, you can end the negative loop of worries and thoughts. (Robinson, 2019)

Research has shown that relaxation techniques can actually change your brain. It provides immediate relief from anxiety and worries if you practice them recurrently. More practicing has a greater impact of relieving anxiety and stress and the more control you will begin to feel over your anxiety and worries.

Speak About Your Worries

An effective way to calm your nervous system and disperse your anxiety is to speak with someone whom you trust – a family member or friend who will listen to you, not judging or criticizing what you are concerned about. When you feel yourself spiraling and your worries seem to want to take control, speaking with them can help to make them less threatening.

Internalizing your worries only makes the buildup of anxiety and worry worse until you feel overwhelmed. However, talking about them aloud can help to put them into perspective. If the worries are really needless, and you verbalize and expose them for what they are, you will be able to have your anxiety and worry levels diminish.

Assemble a strong support group – Gather a few people whom you can trust and whom you feel comfortable with that you know will be there for you and whom you can count on. If you don't have anyone to confide in, building new friendships is a positive option.

Worrying, anxiety and anxious thoughts can encompass your life if you allow them to. Self-examination, developing a worry period, knowing the difference between worry that you can solve and those that you can't, turning to a support group and finding ways to relax and turn off your worry loop are all the ways to manage your worry.

The more you understand what your worries are about and work towards controlling them you will be able to take action to reduce them or letting them go.

Chapter 8: What are the Psychological Triggers? How are they Used?

Emotional triggers. We all have them. Triggers are circumstances or events that may generate psychiatric or emotional symptoms such as discouragement, anxiety, despair, panic or negative self-talk. (Center for Mental Health, 2014)

People reacting to triggers is normal, but they may cause us to spiral downward that makes us feel worse if we don't recognize and respond to them appropriately.

You know the feeling when an emotion trigger crops up. Like when someone makes a comment that is meant as a joke and it's not a big deal. It doesn't bother another person, but it knocks you off balance for the day. Or when someone tells you they are disapproving or disappointed in you. You feel emotionally disrupted and off center and spiral into a period of depression, anxiety, shame or guilt.

If any of this sounds familiar, then you are in need of identifying what your triggers are to understand why you spiral into a negative place.

Identifying what our triggers are can present a challenge, but familiarizing and recognizing and understanding them can help us learn how to better handle them when they are activated, and most importantly, to heal.

Why do we have triggers?

Where do our triggers come from? Why do we all have them? Our childhood has the answers to those questions.

Growing up, we were experiencing pain, suffering, shame or guilt but could not acknowledge or deal with them at the time because we were children. Now, as adults, when we feel a trigger that touches that experience resonating from our childhood and old feeling reemerge, we usually turn towards a way that is by habit or addiction to handle the painful feelings.

When you recognize your triggers, you may contemplate how they originated.

What are your triggers?

When you feel an emotional trigger and the painful feelings that come with it, how are you managing the pain? Are you avoiding them so you won't feel the pain, or are you confronting them? (Paul, 2019)

An example of someone who discovered his trigger and how he is dealing with it.

Bill was raised by an indulgent mother and a father, an attorney, was a very authoritative and regimented man. His father expected Bill to toe the line, study, get good grades and become successful as he was. His father didn't care if he became an attorney, he just wanted Bill to succeed and do him proud. This was his only son who also carried his name. For Bill's father, slacking off and failure weren't options.

Bill rebelled almost from the very beginning of his childhood. His mother, on the other hand, allowed him to express his rebellious side, understanding that he felt pressured and stressed out from his father's expectations. There were many arguments between his parents as to how he should be raised and what should be expected of him.

Bill riled against authority figures. His teachers, when he was in school, reported that he barely attended his classes, his homework was always late, and his grades would barely see him graduate.

Later, as an adult, Bill bristled when anyone made the mistake of telling him what to do.

Even if it was a constructive suggestion meant to be of help to him, he needed to express that he wasn't going to listen or take their advice, even if it was to his benefit to do so. The old adage of *willing to cut his nose off to spite his face* definitely described Bill's attitude towards authority.

Bill became a successful businessman with the help of his mother. Due to his poor grades, he barely graduated high school and he made it very clear he wasn't going to attend college. His mother got him interested in sales, selling advertising space to businesses in their area in a locally published newspaper.

Bill did very well in sales and became a top salesman in at the newspaper. He even developed a segment of advertising that the newspaper had not had very much luck with, but he broke the ice, brought in the new advertisers and was rewarded for his efforts.

There was one problem. Bill did not like authority figures and one night, after an evening out with his guy friends at a local pub, he ran into the ultimate authority figure, the police. He was arrested because he was driving while intoxicated AND because he resisted arrest. He argued with the police officers, tried to break away while they were trying to cuff him and was hit with resisting arrest charges as well as a DUI when he appeared before the judge after a night in jail.

This was a wakeup call for Bill. All that he worked for and how it affected his future. The judge ruled that Bill must attend AA meetings as well as be counseled for the next six months, plus pay a fine. The judge admonished him and reminded Bill it was fortunate that he did not injure or kill anyone while he was DUI. The judge also noted that everyone was subject to be arrested when driving while intoxicated and resisting arrest had not helped the situation.

Bill attended AA meetings and found that his counseling was beneficial. He realized that his resistance to authority figures was due to his childhood trauma and relationship with his father. The constant reprimands by his father, which caused him to rebel each time it happened were triggered when he was stopped by the police and told to follow their rules. When he was arrested and told he was being detained, it brought up the feelings from his childhood and how he reacted was just as he had as a child and later as an adolescent.

Now that he is aware of what his trigger is and how, when he reacts as he did the night of his arrest, it could hurt him in the long run. He continued therapy past the mandatory six months and learned to deal with his trigger from his inner-child emotions in a more compassionate and knowledgable way.

Are any of these triggers familiar to you? The first step to healing and understanding what caused them is to identify them.

- You're rejected by someone (parent(s), sibling, friend)
- Being abandoned by someone or being threatened with their leaving you

- Someone being unavailable
- Being looked upon disapprovingly
- Being shamed or blamed by someone
- Being judged or negatively critiqued by someone
- Being ignored by someone (or a group)
- Someone who tries to control you
- Feeling smothered by someone or their neediness

You can consider the origins of your triggers once you know what they are. If you recognize any of these triggers or are now recalling other triggers not listed that cause you pain, question what from your childhood experiences they might relate to.

You are the only one who can heal your triggers. Take some time to go to the source of the trigger and be compassionate, kind and especially patient - you are dealing with your inner child. (Paul, 2019)

It's not unusual to avoid our triggers when we don't know how they became triggers in the first place. Being unaware only continues to allow the trigger to control you rather than you control it and doesn't help to heal them.

Do any of these techniques apply to how you avoid your triggers? Do you

- Express anger
- Become needy
- Become compliant and a people-pleaser
- Withdraw, distance and shut down from another person

- Lay blame on another person for my pain
- I self-medicate and turn to alcohol and drugs
- I fall back on an addiction – shopping, food, sex, porn, gambling

How do these avoidance techniques make you feel if you can relate to any of them? Realize that because you choose to avoid it and sweep it under the rug, the pain doesn't disappear and you may even feel more pain.

Be honest with yourself and face your triggers. It will help you learn how to be kind and considerate with yourself. Being honest about your triggers and where they came from will heal them in the long run. (Paul, 2019)

Emotional triggers later in life (Plata, 2018)

There are those emotional triggers that manifest in our adulthood. Sadness, anger or envy can very often create a feeling of shame. This emotion comes about because we feel we aren't achieving what we want to and not living up to our potential.

Perfectionism is what activates many of these triggers. When a co-worker is promoted we feel ashamed that we are angry because we may have thought why weren't we good enough to be promoted? Or our best friend is newly engaged to be married and we may feel envious because we don't even have a significant other in our life.

Whatever topic promotes these feelings that are unpleasant, you need to put shame aside. The emotion we should adopt is one of vulnerability. We need to ask ourselves *why do I get angry about another person's opportunities or experiences?* We can begin to recognize our emotional triggers if we ask ourselves this question.

We can take steps to take care of ourselves although we can't avoid all the situations that may provoke emotional triggers. Developing an inner voice that is strong can help us through the situations that make us feel uncomfortable.

We can decide not to expose ourselves to situations that damage our mental health when we discover our emotional triggers. We don't like exposing ourselves to the triggers that can create uncomfortable or unpleasant emotions.

The idea is not to escape from these situations and create a division that separates you from the outer world but becoming aware helps us to learn about our boundaries and limitations and avoid those situations that affect our self-esteem and mental health. (Plata, 2018)

How to discover your emotional triggers

A series of questions can help to discover what your emotional triggers are. It may appear different for each individual but they are revealing in what we can learn about our triggers and how we are affected by them.

A relative or close friend shares exciting news about them. You're happy for them, but feel envious at the same time. What is the news about? Is it a new car? Are they going to be married? Is it a promotion on their job? Are they in a new relationship? Is there a baby on the way?

Are you following someone on a social media site whom you are always comparing their life to yours? Their posts provoke anger in you. What are the things in their posts that incurs the anger? How do you manage your anger?

You're spending time with your friend or family and notice there's a particular topic of conversation that triggers you. What is the topic? When they talk about
X, how do you feel and why?

What can be done about emotionally exposing ourselves to triggers?

There needs to be clarity that there are some people/conversations and/or situations that we can willingly choose to expose them or not, while there are others that are out of our control. Identifying your emotional triggers is that it can make us more aware of our own mental health.

More awareness means we can start to accept responsibility for the manner in which we handle our emotions instead of letting our emotions control us. When we don't manage or process them properly, we end up reacting with others. (Plata, 2018)

It can be extremely difficult for us when someone begins a conversation that is linked to our emotional trigger (remember the trigger is *ours*, not the person who is starting the conversation). It's tough to distance ourselves from our emotions and have a clear thought. However, when this happens, keep this in mind:

The intention of the other person – The person, relative or friend, who is striking your emotional scar may not even be aware of the pain you're experiencing. Keep a fresh viewpoint about the other person's intention. If it's someone who cares about us and our well-being, it is rarely their intention to cause you any pain. Be patient with them, and with yourself, and let them know about your boundaries.

Our pain – Whatever we are feeling, it's significant to understand what it is that we're feeling and is being caused by an actuality in our lives. We really shouldn't run away from what we're feeling, but navigate away from the feeling of shame and totally own them.

Take as much time as you need; you have permission to feel all the feelings but you also need to take responsibility and learn new methods to manage these emotions. If you want to learn how to achieve this, seeking out a psychotherapist who can help you and give you the space to learn how to do this would be beneficial.

We don't know what type of issues or problems other people may be going through and they may be totally unaware of the struggles we are faced with. Let's have patience with people we know care about us and are most often our support system.

They're doing the best they can and if you feel they could do better, come to them in a vulnerable and caring manner and tell them. You may be surprised how open people are in wanting to help someone they care for.

Take advantage of your support system, learn to rely on and trust them. The emotional weight becomes lighter when we have people who are willing to share it. (Plata, 2018)

Secrets of Dark Psychology and How to Use Them

Have you ever felt that you were manipulated into doing something that you really didn't want to do, but ended up doing it anyway?

Is there someone that you know who comes across as really friendly and charming, yet act impulsively, do things that hurt others, but shows no remorse?

Did you ever have a "friend" stop speaking to you without a rational reason, or for no reason at all? You may have said or done something they didn't like and you are now being given the silent treatment. You don't know what you've done but can't find out because you've been shut out from communicating with this person.

Dark psychology is the science and art of mind control and manipulation. It is used by family members, friends, and business associates. It covers cult followings, psychopathy and the darker wishes of others. People use strategies of persuasion, motivation, coercion, and manipulation to attain what they want.

It is the primitive wish in the minds of some humans to control, overpower and overpower others. Dark psychology deals with mental tricks rather than using physical force.

Attributes and behaviors and a list of techniques are used to render control over others. Usually, the person trying to gain control of others have an agenda and use dark psychology for their own self-interest. To get what they want, they will extinguish any obstacle, no matter if it's physical or psychological, to get what they want.

Everyone is a possible target for a psychological assailant. It could be the psychopath who's your spouse, significant other, the neighbor down the street or someone in authority.

The Dark Psychology Triad – In dark psychology the Dark Triad is a reference to what many psychologists and criminologists as the predictor of people who will have problematic, broken relationships as well as displaying criminal behavior.

If someone possesses all three traits, their threat to the rest of society is immediate. Everywhere they go the cause havoc, whether it's at home, school or at work.

The Dark Triad includes the following traits of:

Narcissism – Perceived grandiosity, egotism and a lack of compassion and empathy. They look down on others and may use them to exalt their own image.

This is a characteristic of persons who have narcissistic personality disorders (NPD). They have little or no empathy for others and their lack of empathy may take the form of verbal, psychological or, in some cases, physical abuse. People with NPD are difficult to deal with and most people usually distance themselves from someone who displays this personality disorder.

Machiavellianism – People who deceive and use manipulation, they exploit and abuse others and have zero sense of morality.

Coming from the political dogma of Niccolo Machiavelli who stated that in order to achieve one's political goal, believed that everything is fair game. Machiavellianism is the approach of someone getting what they want as far as their goals and desires using a no holds barred approach.

Although no one wants to be a target of manipulation, it happens more than we think it does. We might not be the target or victim of one of the personalities who are specifically a part of the Dark Triad, but people who are normal, everyday folks who don't necessarily subscribe to this type of psychology have dark psychology imposed on them on a daily basis.

In other words, someone will use any means necessary and will not stop until they get what they want.

Psychopathy – People who come across as friendly and charming but have characteristics that include selfishness, impulsivity, they lack compassion and empathy, and are cold-hearted with no room for remorse.

Psychopathy references an overall set of traits defined by antisocial behavior and is the combination of narcissism, ambition or boldness, Machiavellianism, becoming unhinged and at time obsessive, and cruelty to others.

It is challenging to define as a personality disorder because it can be interchangeable with sociopathy and insanity. This may sound scary, but it's possible that anyone can be a psychopath without your knowing it.

It is obvious from the several traits listed that psychopaths are 10-15% of the inmate population whereas they are only 1% of the general population.

People whose personalities fall into the dark triad and it's being part of the world means that they are walking around in the real world. They stand out in society because of their behavior that can't be hidden from the rest of the population.

If you use dark psychology it doesn't necessarily mean that you are psychopathic by nature. However, many of these techniques are not ones that you want people to know that you use them. You would be looked upon quite differently by family and friends if you decide to use them and if you are found out by someone who knows you.

So, who are the users of dark psychology and how are we affected?

Advertising agencies are pretty much the masters of dark psychology. They persuade, manipulate, motivate and, on occasion, coerce us to buy, buy, buy the products of their clients.

Television, commercial radio, Internet ads, all bombard us and want us to buy. The sales techniques used are numerous. Their client's product is the best made, the best tasting, the product is selling out, whatever the sales pitch, you need to rush out and buy it today.

Salespeople, sales techniques, even the behavior of our superiors is how we face dark psychology. Even children will employ these tactics as they test different behaviors to get what they want. Family members and others whom you love and trust will use dark persuasion and manipulation to get what they want.

Some of the tactics used are:

Lying – Untrue stories, partial truths, exaggeration

Withdrawal – Silent treatment, avoiding someone

Reverse psychology - Asking someone to do something while intending to get them to do the opposite which is what you really wanted

Love flooding – Showing affection for complimenting someone so you can ask them for something or to do something

Love denial - Withholding of affection and attention

Semantic manipulation – In a conversation with a manipulator, you both use words that you assume have a mutual or common meaning. Later, the manipulator says the words have a different meaning to them and their interpretation of the conversation with you is different and they have a different understanding.

Choice restriction – Giving particular choice options that divert from the choice you do not wish someone to make

How Is Dark Psychology Used? Who Uses It?

As stated, dark psychology is being used in a number of ways. When someone uses it and implements it successfully, the target or victim hasn't the slightest idea that they've been attacked and were the object of dark psychology manipulation.

When a person is manipulated into becoming unaware of what's happening, it's easy for the manipulator to attack and control. Rather than thinking they are being controlled, the target believes they have control based on their emotions and beliefs. Someone who is adept at manipulating others will know what these emotions and beliefs are at any time.

The indirect way, or using particular methods by accident is another type of dark psychology. This is more commonly seen in people who would pass a test given for psychopathy. This type of person wants to control someone or need to have it their way.

Desperation or fear are mind tricks that are sometimes used without the person using them being aware that they're actually manipulating the other person. Abusive partners ending a romantic relationship are an example of this type of manipulation.

Dark psychology becomes an illegal or criminal offense. Kidnappings, murders, and cases of abuse can use dark psychology. The victim is usually in contact with the offender for some time. Months or years can pass before anything happens between them.

Over the course of time, the victim's appearance seems different from family and close friends. People feel they know something is not right, but have no way to pinpoint exactly what it is. In the interim, the victim is being conditioned or *programmed* not to talk about the relationship they have with the offender. The offender exists only in the background, freely creating chaos.

Human Psychology and Manipulative Psychology

Having knowledge of human psychology and manipulative psychology is like having a double-edged sword. In the same way, it can be used to do bad things it can also have good things done as an outcome.

Examples of this theory are lying for the purpose of concealing something bad, yet you can lie to be protective of another person. Or, if you use dark psychology to stop an attacker in order to defend ourselves or defending others is also a way that using dark psychology is acceptable.

If a person can persuade or manipulate someone to do something bad, you can persuade or manipulate someone to something good.

While some people use dark psychology tactics and are quite aware of what they're are doing it purposely with the intention of getting what they want, there are those people who are unaware that they are using unethical and dark tactics.

Actually, this is learned behavior from childhood taught to them by their parents. Others learned the techniques while in their teens using the manipulation techniques and found that it worked. They continued to use the techniques so they could get what they wanted.

In certain cases, there is training involved to use manipulation tactics. Sales and marketing training programs typically use dark, unethical persuasion and psychological tactics. These programs are developed to sell a product or create a brand with the purpose of serving their company, a client or themselves and not necessarily the customer.

People who are trained in these programs are convinced that these tactics are okay and the buyer benefits from it. Because, as we all know, the buyers' lives will be so much better when they buy a service or product.

People who use Dark Psychology most often

Sociopaths – True sociopaths (those who meet the clinical definition and diagnosis) are usually intelligent, charming, but also impulsive. They use dark tactics to develop shallow relationships and then take advantage of people

Politicians – Some politicians use dark psychological techniques and dark persuasion to persuade people that they are the right candidate to vote for

Attorneys – Some attorneys concentrate on winning their cases and choose to use dark persuasion techniques to attain the outcome they want

Narcissists – As stated earlier, people who have NPD have self-worth that is inflated and needs validation from others that they are superior. They play to the audience and dream of being adored and worshipped. They use unethical persuasion, and dark manipulation and psychology tactics.

Sales People – This group of people become increasingly focused on achieving a sale (and sales goals) and use dark tactics to persuade and motivate someone to buy their product.

Public Speakers – Some of these people use tactics to increase the emotional state of an audience recognizing it will sell more products at the end of their appearance.

Leaders – The dark tactics they use get higher performance and greater effort from their subordinates.

Selfish people – Anyone who has an agenda and wants things for themselves over others will use any of the dark tactics available.

If you want to know the difference in using persuasive and motivational tactics that are ethical and those that are dark, give it some thought and assess your intent. Are we using the tactics with the intention of helping the other person? If it is then it's fine to use these tactics. However, if it is for your own self-benefit, you can fall into unethical and dark practices.

The goal should be to have a mutually beneficial result. You need to be honest with yourself and really believe that the other person benefits.

We can ask ourselves these questions to evaluate our intention along with our persuasive and motivational tactics:

- Am I approaching this interaction in a good way?
- Who will benefit from this interaction? What is the overall goal of the interaction?
- Am I being fully honest and open?
- Will the other person benefit and will it result as a long-term benefit?
- Will the relationship grow in trust with the other person by my using these tactics?

In order to decide your current tactics for persuasion and motivation, you need to assess yourself if you want to be truly successful in relationships, parenting, work, leadership and other areas in your life.

Approaching and using these tactics in the right way leads to influence and long-term credibility. Approaching it the wrong way by going dark leads to broken relationships, poor character, and long-term failure. People will ultimately see through the darkness and recognize your intent. (Jones, Dr. Jason, 2017)

Conclusion

Thank you for reading Overcoming Social Anxiety: *A Step by Step Guide and Proven Techniques on How to Use Psychological Triggers and Dark* Psychology *Secrets to Understand How to Stop Worrying and Stop Anxiety* to the end.

Many people don't read through an entire book. They are interested and intrigued by the title and the description of its contents when they first purchase it and begin to read it. Then some distraction has them put it down and move on to other activities.

It appears that you are serious about learning about social anxiety disorder and its effects on the people who suffer from it. Possibly you or someone you know, a family member or a friend, who is affected and wants to learn more about it. It also outlines the signs and symptoms of the disorder and how it affects the people who have SAD.

Before you read this book, you may have thought that social anxiety disorder was not a very serious condition and the most it affected was someone getting anxious or stressed. It doesn't occur to people who don't have this condition that people with SAD suffer from fear, depression, and self-medicate with alcohol or drugs.

Now that you have learned more about this mental condition and its effects, you are better equipped to better understand a person with this disorder.

Hopefully, this book is informative as well as a guide and you will send me an email and let me know how you've benefited from this book.

CPSIA information can be obtained
at www.ICGtesting.com
Printed in the USA
BVHW070132230221
600781BV00003B/252